APOSTOLIC & PROPHETIC DICTIONARY

LANGUAGE OF THE END-TIME CHURCH

ABRAHAM S RAJAH

WESTBOW
PRESS
A DIVISION OF THOMAS NELSON

Unless otherwise indicated, Scripture is taken from the New King James Version (NKJV). Copyright ©1982 by Thomas Nelson, Inc. Used by permission. New King James Version.

WestBow Press books may be ordered through booksellers or by contacting:

WestBow Press
A Division of Thomas Nelson
1663 Liberty Drive
Bloomington, IN 47403
www.westbowpress.com
1 (866) 928-1240

ISBN: 978-1-4908-1963-1 (sc)
ISBN: 978-1-4908-1962-4 (hc)
ISBN: 978-1-4908-1964-8 (e)

Library of Congress Control Number: 2013922225

Printed in the United States of America.

WestBow Press rev. date: 12/12/2013

APOSTOLIC & PROPHETIC DICTIONARY

by Abraham S. Rajah

Apostolic & Prophetic Handbook Series (the God Wants You To ... Series):

Vol. 1   *Prophetic Handbook: God Wants You to Prophesy: (5 Steps to Get You Prophesying)*

Vol. 2   *Deliverance Handbook: God Wants You to Cast out Demons and Live Demon-Free*

Vol. 3   *Healing Handbook: God Wants You to Heal the Sick and Live in Healing*

Vol. 4   *Prosperity Handbook: God Wants You to Prosper and Prosper Others*

Vol. 5   *Signs and Wonders Handbook: God Wants You to Move in Signs and Wonders*

Training by Equipping, Activating, and Releasing (TEAR Programme) Series

Vol. 1   *Believers Handbook*

Vol. 2   *Leaders Handbook*

Vol. 3   *Ministers Handbook*

To God and His end-time army of kings and priests.

To the fathers and mothers in the faith who have pioneered movements and stood against traditions and norms. You brought us what is fresh and cutting edge as you heard from the Holy Spirit, and this work was made possible by your courage. You are the men and women of God that have brought the words in this book to life.

To my three soldiers, Abigail, Elijah, and Zion Abraham.

CONTENTS

Words of Thanks/ Acknowledgements

I am grateful to my wife for her support and encouragement and for her assistance in the word processing and proofreading of the manuscript.

To my three little soldiers, who often bore the sacrifice of my long hours spent writing, I salute you.

To my editing team, apostle Motumi Motseari and Rodney Reddy, your efforts are a large contributing factor to this piece of work.

To the army of kings and priests that God is raising all over the world, I say only this: Arise, for His return is near.

I release this into your hands with the prayer that God will use you and that your purpose in life will be seen to impact others.

Abraham S. Rajah
Sandton, Gauteng,
South Africa

INTRODUCTION

What do you get when you combine the most relevant truths in the church today with easy-to-understand explanations? You get the dictionary you are now holding – the *Apostolic & Prophetic Dictionary*. Based on scriptural foundations, its purpose is to provide essential biblical truths that will empower even the most beginning believer to a higher dimension of the Holy Spirit's revelation.

The Church of Jesus Christ is rising with a different type of people; these are the people that hear God and His voice, and they are speaking a different language, the *language of revelation and truth*.

God, who cannot be expressed in human words, has spoken and is still speaking, revealing certain key truths and phrases of revelation. Using extensive research methods featuring the language of *apostolic and prophetic pioneers* from around the world, this dictionary promises to be fresh and cutting edge.

In this dictionary you will find a *glossary of vocabulary and terminology* that every believer, who desires to be part of the *apostolic and prophetic people* and *restoration*, must come to know. God is raising up these people in these last days.

These terms will commonly be used in the final move of the Holy Spirit as we prepare for the coming of our King. This final move is the *apostolic and prophetic movement*, or *restoration*, to be seen and manifested through the *kings and priests* of God.

The key to the *Apostolic & Prophetic Dictionary* is its combination of simplicity and depth. For example, although some of the words and phrases have been explained from the Greek or Hebrew (because I believe it gives a richer meaning), this has been done carefully so as not to overwhelm the reader with too much information, as is often the style of an exhaustive concordance such as *Strong's*.

AUTHOR'S NOTE
(PLEASE READ)

Some of the entries in the dictionary follow the word 'see' where the definition should be given. This highlights that they have been explained under the word or phrase mentioned after the 'see'. For example,

Spiritual Gifts: See **Gifts of the Spirit**

Another handy feature is the insertion of 'see also', which appears at the end of some explanations. This is an indispensable connection of interrelated words or phrases which has been developed for the reader or researcher to obtain a richer meaning or deeper understanding.

Words that appear **bolded** within the body of one explanation highlight that the word or phrase has been explained in the dictionary either on its own or within the body of another definition. It also highlights that the reader is encouraged to take a look.

The *Scriptures* explaining the phrase or words have been put either in the middle of the text (if directly) or at the end (if generally relevant). It is the responsibility of the researcher to search the Word for a deeper revelation and understanding of the word or phrase.

The *language choice* is that of the UK and South African English. Hence, some spelling may differ. For example: honor – honour; favor – favour; checks – cheques. My American and other differing English-style readers, please take note of this.

It is worth noting that although some of the words in this dictionary apply in the *context* of the Bible and the secular world, I have chosen to confine them mainly within the context of the Word or kingdom of God.

It is also worth noting that I have used *creative license* and have chosen to write 'satan' without a capital S in the text (some entries require capitalization, but not when I'm referring directly to satan). This is because I do not deem him worthy of such an honour.

-A-

Abraham's Blessings refers to the type of blessings God gave Abraham, especially the ones mentioned in Deut. 28: 1–13. This blessing is the *empowerment or anointing given to Abraham and eventually to all believers to prosper in every area of their lives.* All believers are the **seeds of Abraham,** which means when someone becomes born again, he or she is taken by God as the descendant or offspring of Abraham and is worthy of all the promises God gave to Abraham and his seed (Gal. 3: 8, 15, 29). The blessing is stronger and more powerful than any curse. Believers must meditate on this truth and speak it into every area of their lives. Abraham's blessing is part of **the blessing** of the Lord, which is 'the empowerment to bring back all that God had given to believer shad and lost in the garden of Eden' (Gen. 1: 26–31).

The opposite of the blessing is the **curse of the law,** and this is 'the empowerment to fail and to be cursed in every area of life'. The curse brings with it poverty, lack, sickness, defeat, fear, etc. All those who have become **born again** have been spiritually released or **redeemed from the curse of the law.** This means Jesus has fulfilled all the requirements of the laws of God against mankind. However, this reality must be brought into the natural by *faith* and the Word *(*Gen. 1: 26–31, 28: 4; Deut. 28; Prov. 10: 22; Gal. 3: 13–14*).* See also **Power to Prosper** and **Prosperity.**

Acting on the Word: See **Acts/Actions of Faith.**

Activating the Supernatural: See **Supernatural.**

Activation: This refers to the 'act of triggering' or 'stirring up' a gift or gifts within a believer in order for him or her to move in the grace of that gift or gifts. When activation is done, it releases the believer to move in that gift. Believers can be activated to speak in **tongues,** prophesy, operate in gifts of **healing, deliverance, power to prosper, signs and wonders,** etc. **Spiritual gifts** are given by the Holy Spirit according to 1 Cor. 12: 4–11 and Rom. 12: 6–8, but they are activated by faith within the believer. Activation can come in several ways, such as by attending a service or conference where the gift is practiced, during a time of **prayer** or **meditation,** by listening to or reading certain material, or by receiving prayer or **laying on of hands** by a believer who moves in that gift (Rom. 1: 11; 2 Tim. 1: 6). See also **Impartation; Supernatural.**

Acts/Actions of Faith: This refers to actions intentionally done by a believer as a sign of his or her faith in God and His Word. It can also be called **acting on the Word.** Examples may include sowing financial seeds in hard times, opening a new business bank account when a business is declared bankrupt, waking up early and washing as if going to work, even though unemployed, etc. A **leap of faith** is similar but may refer more specifically to a big decision made by a believer as an act of faith. Examples include moving to a different country, cancelling a scheduled medical operation, etc. See also **Point of Contact; Faith; Standing on the Word.**

Adonai: See **Names of God.**

Adoption: See **Sons of God.**

Adultery: See **Sexual Immorality.**

Ambassadors: This refers to the position believers have been given to act on behalf of God on earth. It comes from the Greek word *presbeuo*, which means someone who is mature, trustworthy, and respected to act as a representative. All believers as ambassadors are representatives of the **kingdom of God** on earth. They are governed by the Word of God and have a responsibility to bring about that Word on earth. This is part of **who we are in Christ Jesus** (2 Cor. 5: 20; Eph. 6: 19–20).

Amen: This word means surely, truly, indeed, or let it be so. When believers say amen, they are calling the spiritual to become natural. It is a powerful word of faith to claim finality to whatever God has said and promised in His Word (2 Cor. 1: 20; Rev. 3: 14). See also **Faith Confessions/Decrees/Declarations; Faith; Prayer.**

Amillennialism: See **Millennial Era.**

Angelic Ministry: This refers to all ways in which **angels,** God-created spirit beings or messengers, serve believers and God in order to fulfil the plans and purpose of God. Angels are servants to believers. This is because believers are higher in creation than angels because we are created in the very image of God. Angels can come to strengthen, feed, fight for, protect, provide for, or deliver messages for believers. Angelic ministry must be welcomed and expected by believers. God releases this type of ministry more and more, and believers should expect the reality of this ministry in their lives (2 Kings 6: 15–17; Acts 10: 3–7; 27: 23–24; Heb. 1: 7, 14). See also **Demons/Satan; Visitation.**

Angels: See **Angelic Ministry.**

Anointed: See **Anointing.**

Anointing refers to the *ability or empowerment of the Holy Spirit to do what cannot be done by human effort.* The anointing comes to bring the manifestation of the Word of God in any area. The word **anoint** is 'mashach' in Hebrew, which means to 'pour, rub, smear, or set aside' for God by using anointing oil. In the Bible, people and objects were anointed to consecrate or set them apart for God to use *(Ex. 29: 29, 30: 25–29; 1 Sam. 16: 13).* Anointing oil is a symbol of the Holy Spirit and His enabling power and presence (1 Sam. 16: 13; Acts 10: 38). The anointing is therefore the Holy Spirit rubbing Himself or pouring Himself on a believer in order to express or show Himself through the believer. In a *physical sense,* it can mean to pour, rub, or smear oil, but in a *spiritual sense,* it means to empower or come upon a believer. The anointing can be stored in physical objects and transferred (for example, in and through clothing, handkerchiefs, water, oil, etc.) (Acts 19: 11–12; James 5: 14–15).

To be **anointed** means 'to be set apart by God in order to be used in a certain way or to display or show a certain way the Holy Spirit operates'. **Unction of the Holy Spirit** is similar to the meaning of anointing. It comes from the Greek word *'chrisma'* meaning *an anointing* or *an empowerment* to do something. The unction of the Holy Spirit is used more specifically used to refer to the inner conviction to act, say or do something as a result of the anointing of the Holy Spirit on a believer's life. (1 John 2:20).

Christ is *Hamashiach* in Hebrew, meaning the *Anointed One*; it is not the surname of the Lord Jesus but a name to describe His ministry on earth.

There are two broad categories where the anointing is found: **personal anointing,** which is the anointing upon an individual, and

corporate anointing, which is the anointing found only when two or more gather. See also **Activation; Impartation.**

Antichrist Spirit: See **Antichrist.**

Anointing You Respect Is the Anointing You Attract: This phrase simply means the anointing, or more specifically the gifting, teachings, and callings that a believer admires and honours on another believer is the same and will be imparted upon his or her own life. See also **Honouring a Man or Woman of God; Impartation; Sowing into Anointing.**

Antichrist: This refers to one man who will rise to become the leader of the world. He will have supernatural powers given to him by satan. He will be defeated by Christ at His **Second Coming**. The antichrist will be responsible for the **abomination of desolation,** which is believed by scholars to be the time that he claims to be God Almighty (Dan. 9: 27, 11: 31, 12: 11; Mark 13: 14).

The **antichrist spirit** is any spirit that opposes the truth of the Word or **kingdom of God** (2 Thess. 2: 3–11; 1 John 2: 18; Rev. 13). See also **Eschatology.**

Apostle: This is one of the fivefold ministries and a foundational office, according to Eph. 2: 20 and 4: 11 and 1 Cor. 12: 28. This word is *apostolos* in the Greek, meaning 'sent one', or 'one who is sent'. It is an office entrusted by Jesus to establish and correct **doctrine**, plant churches, oversee churches, pioneer new truths, impart and activate gifts and callings in others, network and form **apostolic teams,** and **equip** believers to perform their **membership role.** The anointing, gifts, or grace that accompany apostles are usually **special faith, healings, miracles, deliverance, and authority** for opening **spiritual realms** for the kingdom to be established, etc.

As the forerunner and pioneering office, apostles have the grace to **bind strongholds** in order for the **kingdom of God** to be built on earth. **False apostles** are *unsent* by Jesus (Rev. 2: 20). They do not pursue the objectives of the true Word of God; instead, they are driven by **false doctrine**, selfish ambition, and sometimes satanic powers (1 Cor. 4: 15; 2 Cor. 11: 1–4, 28; Eph. 3: 5). See also **Activation; Fatherhood; Fivefold Ministry; Impartation.**

Apostle/Prophet in the Marketplace: This term may refer to two things:

(1) A believer who is an **apostle** or **prophet** in which a priestly or church setting is the believer's main area of influence, but he or she may also exert influence in the marketplace.

(2) It also refers to a believer who functions in the anointing, gifts, or grace of an apostle or prophet but is called into the marketplace and not the church. The latter is the most common definition used today. Joseph, Daniel, and Esther in the Bible are examples of this type of believer. See also **Kings and Priests.**

Apostolic and Prophetic: This generally refers to any activity associated with the **apostolic and prophetic gifts** and principles. More specifically, when it is said that something or someone is **apostolic,** it means it or the person displays the functions, values, or characteristics that are in line with the office of the apostle. When it is said that something or someone is **prophetic,** it means it or the person somehow communicates the heart and mind of God. This can be information from the past, present, or future, given meaning through the prophetic gifts. See also **Apostle; Apostolic Believer/ Minister; Prophet; Prophetic Believer/Minister.**

Apostolic/Prophetic Networks: These are different **apostolic and prophetic ministries** with common beliefs and visions who group themselves in order to support and pray for one another, share resources and material, and have oversight for accountability over each other. These networks often set up conventions and conferences together. Networks are established to have a larger and more effective impact in their regions and nations.

Apostolic and Prophetic Covering: See **Covering.**

Apostolic and Prophetic Leadership refers to the ability to lead others by using the gifts and principles that come with the office of the **apostle** and **prophet**. One of the key characteristics of this type of leadership is the laying down of **present** and **new truths**. This is what the Bible calls the **foundation of the apostles and prophets** (Eph. 2: 20). See also **Fatherhood; Leadership.**

Apostolic and Prophetic Ministries: This refers to ministries that teach and practice the apostolic and prophetic principles and gifts. See also **Apostle; Apostolic Gifts; Prophet; Prophetic Gifts.**

Apostolic and Prophetic Order: This is the structure and order to be followed in the Body of Christ according to 1 Cor. 12: 28. This structure emphasizes the need for mature and trained apostles and prophets to have the primary **prophetic insight** and **apostolic oversight** in all churches.

Prophetic insight refers to the need of every local church to have either internal or external prophets to regularly provide *guidance* and *revelation* on the overall nature and state of the church.

The *apostolic oversight* is the need for every local church to have *covering, oversight,* and *accountability* to apostles. It also has the meaning of believers being trained and released by apostles and prophets or apostolic and prophetic leaders. A **local church,** for example, cannot be started without **God's timing** and **God's release**. This timing and release is communicated to the believer by God, but it is confirmed and given oversight and insight by apostles and prophets as in the New Testament church. All churches and pastors need to follow this order as it promotes accountability and stability within the church. It also prevents leaders from being an authority unto themselves. The order can be achieved for example through **partnering** and **spiritual mentoring**. See also **Covering; Commissioning; Ordination.**

Apostolic and Prophetic Pioneers: This term refers to **apostles** and **prophets** who establish **new truths** in the church. These pioneers often go against existing traditions and teachings within the church in order to establish or restore a new truth from the Holy Spirit and the Word. As a result, they often face much criticism and persecution. They often form foundations for new revelations and movements for all other believers to follow (1 Cor. 12: 28; Eph. 2: 20; 3: 5). See also **Present Truths; Restoration.**

Apostolic and Prophetic Teams: This refers to two or more people who are sent in order to make an impact by using the **apostolic and prophetic** principles and gifts. God is raising more and more of these teams to bring about a larger impact into the world. These teams are not necessarily commissioned or ordained by their elders (Matt. 1–5; Luke 10: 1–3). See also **Apostolic and Prophetic Networks; Commissioning; Ordination.**

Apostolic Believer/Minister: This refers to someone who moves or functions in the anointing or gifts that accompany the **apostle** without being called as an apostle.

Apostolic Gifts: This refers to the gifts of the Holy Spirit that accompany the office of the **apostle** and **apostolic believers**. These may include **deliverance, power, miracles, signs and wonders,** wisdom, **and training.**

Apostolic Mandate: See **Apostolic Strategy.**

Apostolic Oversight: See **Apostolic and Prophetic Order.**

Apostolic Strategy refers to the overall manner, tact, and skill needed and used by apostles and apostolic ministers to fulfil the **apostolic mandate**. This mandate includes but is not limited to **identifying gifts and callings, equipping** believers to fulfil their **membership role** in the Church, establishing correct **doctrine** and exposing **false doctrine**, activating and imparting believers in the apostolic gifts, advancing the **kingdom of God** in all nations, etc. Apostles are strategists in that they are able to build on earth according to the blueprints they receive regularly from heaven. Building God's kingdom by using the tact and plans of an apostolic mind-set is called **apostolic wisdom**. See also **Apostle.**

Apostolic Wisdom: See **Apostolic Strategy.**

Area of Influence/Calling: This refers to a certain people and place that a believer is called to influence, impact, and transform. This area is determined by God. The area of influence can be communities, districts, a nation or nations, and even continents. Finding the area of influence is one of the keys to moving in effective ministry because it is aligned to the will of God. This also avoids taking up someone else's calling. *No believer is called everywhere, but every believer is called somewhere.* See also **Calling.**

Armageddon: This refers to the battle that is to take place between Jesus and the **antichrist,** resulting in the defeat of the antichrist and his armies. The battle is believed to occur in a place called *Megiddo* in Israel (Rev. 16: 16). See also **Eschatology; Millennial Era.**

Army of the Lord: This refers to a group of believers called from the Church who form God's end-time army. This army has been prophesied to make more impact for God than any other generation before it according to Joel 2: 2. Any believer can be a part of this army if he or she wants to. This is done by simply asking the Lord, Jesus, who is the commander of the army, to enlist him or her. There is no limit to the number of believers in this army. This army will mainly show itself in the **kings and priests** model (Isa. 13: 1–13; Jer. 51: 20–23; Joel 2: 1–11).

Ascension Gifts: See **Fivefold Ministry.**

Assignment: See **Calling.**

Authority: This word comes from the Greek word *exousia*. It means 'delegated or conferred authority', or 'authority that is given to another'. It can also mean 'leave', or 'permission to exercise dominion, jurisdiction, rulership, leadership, or the influence of another with higher authority'. The authority of Jesus Christ is the highest authority in heaven, on earth, and beneath the earth (Phil. 2: 8–11). Jesus as the source of all authority has given believers His authority. This means Jesus has given us the right to exert His rule on the earth and over satan. Authority gives believers the right to display the power, or *dunamis,* of God. Believers who are submitted under authority will display the greatest authority themselves. Just as Jesus submitted to the Father to receive all authority, even so believers must submit to Jesus and His **apostolic and prophetic order** in order to move in the highest manifestation of His authority (Matt. 28: 18–20; Luke 10: 19).

- B -

Babylon System: This refers to a world centred system that is based on man's reliance on their flesh and wisdom. This phrase is taken from the tower of Babel attempt in Gen. 11. It is a system that places its trust not on the Word of God but on human strength and at times satanic powers. Babylon is depicted in the Rev. 16–18 as a demonic spirit that influences many nations to unite and act against God's kingdom and Word. Believers can successfully oppose this system by manifesting the kingdom of God as ambassadors of Christ. God has guaranteed its destruction and all those who support it. *See* also **Antichrist Spirit; Kingdom of Darkness; Seven Mountain Kingdoms.**

Backslider: This refers to a believer who has backslidden or has stopped or lost interest in following the principles of the Word of God. Such believers usually have lost their love for God and the things that please Him. Jesus can save to the uttermost and longs to see all backsliders return to Him (James 4: 8–10; 2 Pet. 2: 20–22; 1 John 1: 9; Rev. 2: 4–5). See also **Carnal Believer/Christian**

Baptism: This word comes from the Greek word *baptizo* which means 'to immerse'. There are two kinds of baptism that the Bible mentions.

(1) **Water baptism,** which is the immersion of a believer into water, symbolising the washing away of the sin-full nature

and the death of their old ways. The process of going down and under the water also represents dying with Christ, while rising from the water represents being made alive or resurrected in Him with His *zoe* life (Rom. 6: 4; Col. 2: 11–12). The Bible commands all believers to be baptised with water. This should be done at least once but can be done repeatedly by faith as an act of recommitment to God (Matt. 28: 19; Acts 2: 38, 41; 1 Pet. 3: 21).

(2) **Baptism with the Holy Spirit** is the in-filling of the believer with His presence and power which is evidenced with the **gifts of the Spirit**, and especially the **gifts of tongues**. This process is the next step after a believer becomes **born again**. At the time of being born again the Holy Spirit comes to *indwell*, but when asked by faith the Holy Spirit can come to *infill* the believer. This baptism of the Holy Spirit is also called the **baptism with fire** because fire is symbolic of the Holy Spirit (Matt. 3: 11). Every believer should be in filled by the Holy Spirit in order to enjoy a richer walk with God, and to demonstrate His kingdom (Acts 1: 4–5, 19: 1–6).

Believer: This refers to any person who has received the Lord Jesus Christ as their personal sacrifice for sin by saying and meaning the **salvation prayer**. They believe in Him as Lord, Saviour and the only way to God and to heaven. A believer also relies on the Bible as the highest authority of truth on the earth. (John 3: 16–17; 14: 6; 17: 17; Rom. 10: 9–10) *See* also **Salvation; Sinner's prayer**

Bishop: This word comes from the Greek word *episkopos* and it refers to an *overseer* of a **local church**. Generally speaking anyone who oversees a local church can qualify to be called a bishop, provided they meet the requirements given by the apostle Paul in 1 Timothy

3: 1–4 and Titus 1: 7–9. As a result of these requirements it has become common in the Church for other ministers to recognize and call other believer's into the title of bishop, by recognising their fruit and works in the ministry.

Body of Christ: This refers to the entire body of believers who are the extension of Jesus Christ with Him as the head. The word Body is used to refer to the believer's type of connection to Jesus. It is a symbolic comparison of the Church to a human body. As a human body has different parts with different functions, even so all believers form different parts of the Body of Christ with different roles to play in His Church. Every part of this body has a **membership ministry** or **role** to play, which is the unique calling, ministry or role that God has placed on a believer in order to benefit the Body of Christ. This is usually done by a believer **serving in the house** or their own **local church**. All believers must attempt to serve in their local church (1 Cor. 12: 12–27; Eph. 1: 20–23; Col. 1: 18). See also **Calling**

Boldness: See **Supernatural Boldness.**

Bondages: See **Strongholds**

Born Again: It literally means to be 'born from above'. The state of being born again refers to the recreation of the *sinful human spirit* in order to become like the *sinless nature of God*. In order to become born-again a person must use their words to confess their sinful nature to God and believe in their heart that Jesus Christ has been raised from the dead by God and is now their Lord and Saviour (Rom. 10: 9–10). Being born again is the only way in which a person can be accepted by God and receive anything from Him. This new nature is also called the **new creation/creature**. This reborn spirit also called the **divine nature** has the ability to function like God and God Himself lives in it. The Bible also calls it the **new man.** (John 3: 3–7; Rom. 3: 23; 1 Cor. 6: 19; 2 Cor. 5: 17–21; Eph. 4: 24; Col. 3: 10). See also **Believer; Salvation; Sin; Sinner's Prayer.**

Breakthrough: This refers to the end or an interruption to a period of trials in a believer's life, resulting in some form of answered prayer or an epiphany, therefore providing relief from an on-going challenging situation. See also **Trials/Tests/Tribulations/ Sufferings; Wilderness experience/Period.**

Calling: This refers to the specific purpose for which a believer was born as given by God. It is often referred to as the **will of God**. God has called every believer for a specific and a unique calling, and it is obedience and faithfulness to this calling that will determine the rewards we receive in heaven from God (1 Cor. 3: 12–15; Rev. 22: 12). Every believer that desires to spend eternity with God must seek this calling with all of their heart and then depend on **grace** in order to accomplish it. The calling of God is accompanied by certain **gifts of the Holy Spirit** which are tools to accomplish or fulfil the calling. The **general calling** or **general will of God** refers to the requirements that God places on all believers. For example all must gather in church services, all can marry only one other believer, all must sow financially and so on. This general will is found in the written Word or *logos*. The **specific calling** or **specific will of God** refers to the exact details that God wants to accomplish on earth using a believer. For example the specific will of God will direct a person where to attend the service, which believer to marry and where to sow financially. The specific will of God is found in the *rhema* or revealed word which God gives to believers. (Jer. 29: 11–13; 2 Tim. 1: 9). The calling can also relate to the **assignment** or **mandate** of God for a believer. This often refers to the specific task that God has given a believer to accomplish for a specific time or **season**. Often many assignments will form part of the calling of God. The faithfulness we display in one assignment or mandate will result in a higher mandate or assignment. (Acts 13: 2; Rom. 11: 29; Eph. 4: 1; 2 Tim. 4: 5) *See also* **Message; Ministry.**

Carnal Believer/Christian: Also called a worldly or lukewarm believer. It refers to someone who is **born again** but lives according to the desires of their flesh. Such believers are often not serious about God or His will and purpose for their lives and live as they choose. The Bible warns very sternly against this type of believer and calls them lukewarm (Matt. 5: 13; 1 Cor. 3: 1–3; 2 Pet. 2: 20–22; 1 John 2: 15–16; Rev. 3: 15–16). See also **Backslider.**

Celibacy: This refers to the grace given to a believer to remain unmarried and sexually inactive. Married believers cannot exercise this option because the Bible is clear that married couples must have regular sexual intimacy. The apostle Paul had this grace on his life (1 Cor. 7: 7–9).

Cessationism: This is a **false doctrine** that teaches that the **gifts of the Holy Spirit** stopped working through believers, from the time of the early Church and the first apostles. It teaches that such gifts were only necessary for the establishment of the early Church and that once it was established the gifts ceased to operate. See also **Activation; Anointing; Impartation; Supernatural**

Character: This refers to the *nature, traits, qualities, of a person that is seen in his or her actions, behaviours, and words.* The character of a believer is more important to God than the gifts or anointing upon their life. This is because *gifts are given* and *character is developed* within a person. This can only be done with a believer yielding to God over long periods of time. It is the character of a believer that will sustain their gifts and not the other way around. This is why the apostle Paul emphasized the need for proven characters in places of leadership and not their gifts. **God makes the man before the ministry** is a term commonly used by Dr. Bill Hamon, a major **apostolic and prophetic pioneer,** to mean that God places a lot more emphasis on the character and spiritual maturity of a believer before sending them out into wide public ministry. The bigger the impact of the ministry given by God, than the longer and more intense the character building period will be according to Luke 12: 48 (Matt. 7: 20; Rom. 5: 3–4; 1 Tim. 3: 1–12; Titus 1: 5–9). See also **Bishop; Deacon; Fruit of the Spirit; Spiritual Maturity.**

Charismatic movement: See **Movement.**

Christ: See **Anointing.**

Church Planting: This refers to the starting and establishment of new **local churches.** Church planting is usually done by **apostles** or **apostolic ministers.** Although not strictly necessary, there is usually a main or **parent** local church from which the others come from. These new churches are also known as **branches.** Church planting involves **winning souls, training** them, and then placing them into positions where they can be used by God (Acts 14: 21–23).

Church: This word comes from the Greek word *ekklesia* and means 'those that are called out of and into' or the 'called out ones'. This word church can be used in three main ways:

(1) The universal Body of Jesus Christ, also call the **universal church;**

(2) The individual who believes in Jesus Christ, also called the individual church; and

(3) A building or place where believers gather to have a service, also called a **local church** (Matt. 16: 18; Acts 9: 31). See also **Body of Christ.**

Closed Vision/Closed-Eye Vision: See **Vision.**

Coming soon: See **Prepare the Way.**

Commissioning: This refers to the **sending out** of a believer by elders in order to accomplish their **membership role**. This is usually a role of leadership. Being commissioned is a physical step with a spiritual purpose, because with it comes the **spiritual covering** of the elders. In truth all believers have been commissioned by Jesus to witness to the lost and demonstrate His power as given in Mark 16: 15. This is known as the **Great Commission**. However commissioning of believers by elders is an orderly way by recognizing their gifts of a person and then releasing them to function in those gifts under oversight. It is usually done through prayer and by the **laying on of hands** of the elders. Being sent is different from being **sent-out**. The former happens when an elder sends out believers usually in teams to various places (for example streets, schools, villages etc.) in order to witness and demonstrate the power of God (Num. 27: 18–23; Matt. 28: 18–20; Acts 13: 2–4). See also **Apostolic and Prophetic Order; Membership Ministry; Ordination; Prophetic Presbytery.**

Compassion/Mercy: This is one of the gifts of the Holy Spirit mentioned in Rom. 12: 8. It is the ability given to a believer to show compassion or have great mercy for the needs of others. It can also be called the **gift of compassion/ mercy**. This type of gift or ministry often results in the involvement of a believer in *orphanages, shelters, feeding schemes*, giving *medical attention, visiting and tending for the sick,* *imprisoned or elderly*. Although all believers are called to show mercy or compassion some have this grace on their lives more than others (Matt. 25: 35–36; Luke 6: 35–40).

Condemnation: See **Conviction of the Holy Spirit.**

Conviction of the Holy Spirit: This refers to the gentle communication given by God within the believer to indicate that He disapproves of certain actions or behaviour. The opposite of this voice is **condemnation** which is a harsh, loud and attacking voice of satan and his demons, on the mind of a believer intended to cause guilt and shame. satan is an accuser and his condemnation is always intended to point out failures and wrongs (Rev. 12: 10). The conviction of God is always given in order to produce Godly sorrow and lead the believer to **repentance**, and to restore them to the path of His perfect will (Rom. 2: 4). Believers must learn to discern these two voices in order to avoid unnecessary thoughts of shame and guilt. Jesus did not come to condemn us but to bring His salvation and righteousness. All sins that are confessed are forgiven by God (John 12: 47; Rom. 8: 1; 2 Cor. 5: 7; 1 John 1: 9). See also **Receptive to the Holy Spirit.**

Corporate Anointing: See **Anointing.**

Covenant: A covenant can be defined as an agreement reached by two parties by the shedding of blood. The word *covenant* is *berith* in the Hebrew and *diatheke* in Greek. Both of these words mean 'to cut' and have the meaning of blood flowing. Blood is necessary in order for a covenant to be established. Covenants were regularly practiced in the Bible as a form of two parties uniting together for a common purpose. A covenant is a very serious agreement that cannot be broken. God has had two main covenants with mankind, the **Old** and the **New covenant**. The old covenant applied to God and the Jewish people. The New covenant applies to all who become **born again**, regardless of age, sex, race, or nationality. God will never break any covenant He makes. Believers must understand the serious nature of a covenant in the Bible and trust God to fulfil all the promises in the New Covenant in Jesus Christ (Gen. 21: 22–34; Heb. 9: 22; 10; 1–22).

Covering: This refers to the **spiritual covering** or protection over a person or ministry. Covering is usually provided for by ministries or ministers who have matured in ministry and have been given **authority** in the **spiritual realm** by God. **Apostolic and prophetic covering** refers to the covering offered by **apostolic and prophetic ministries**. Covering can be obtained through submission under a ministry. It can also be obtained through service and obedience to the ministry or its leaders; also by sowing financially and through prayer from the covering ministry. Only ministries who are matured and confirmed by God can qualify to cover others. This is because God has tested and proven them. Covering is used for two main reasons:

(1) To receive the gifts, grace or anointing flowing from the head ministry and;

(2) to receive protection from spiritual attacks. See also **Apostolic and Prophetic Order; Networking; Partnership**.

Covetousness: See **Idolatry**.

Creative Miracles: This refers to when God supernaturally creates something that was not there before, or was there but not functioning as it should. It can include human body parts, food, water, building material, money etc. This type of miracle falls within the broader category of miracles as a gift of the Holy Spirit, and believers can trust God to move in it just as any other gift (Matt. 14: 13–20; 15: 30–39). See also **Gift of Miracles.**

Crucifying the Flesh: See **Lusts of the Works/Sins/Lusts of the Flesh**

Curse of the Law: See **Abraham's Blessing.**

-D-

Day of the Lord: See **End Times.**

Deacon: This word comes from the Greek word *diakonos*, which means 'servant' or 'waiting man'. Deacons usually serve as subordinates to a **pastor** or **bishop**. There are requirements placed on this position by the Bible according to 1 Tim. 3: 8–12. See also **Bishop.**

Debauchery/Lasciviousness: It means given to lust or expressing lust. It is also called **lewdness**. It refers to an uncontrolled desire to engage in sensual pleasures (Gal. 5: 19–21 King James Version). See also **Works/Sins/Lusts of the flesh; Sexual Immorality.**

Deliverance Minister: See **Deliverance.**

Deliverance Ministry*:* See **Deliverance.**

Demon/Devil Consciousness: This refers to the mind-set of a believer that makes him or her more aware of the existence of demons and the devil and the potential danger they may cause, resulting in **fear**. This is different from **God/Word consciousness** which is the mind-set of a believer that makes him or her more aware of the existence of God His promises and goodness, resulting in **faith**. In as much as believers should have knowledge of **satan** or **demons**, this must never result in being fascinated or obsessed with the existence or study of demons, to the point of thinking about them for a majority of the time. However it is also wrong to completely neglect the existence of devils, as this is will result in ignorance and unnecessary attacks from the enemy. The believer should be more God conscious as this will result in His presence, guidance and protection (Phil. 4: 8). See also **Meditation.**

Demonic/Forbidden Practices: This refers to activities and beliefs that are prohibited by God in His Word. Believers should stay away from these type of activities as they invite demonic spirits which cause destruction and even death. These practices are **demonic doorways,** or open doors that give satan a legal right to enter into the life of a person. Some of these practices include

(1) Human and animal sacrifices

(2) **Divination,** which is the practice of inquiring into the future by using demonic powers. *Psychics, fortune tellers, séances, mediums, soothsayers, diviners, spiritists* etc. use divination. These people often make use of *Ouija boards, astrology, horoscopes, numerology, tea leaves, palm,* and *tarot card readings* etc. in order to receive and give information. Any form of communication to God other than through the Bible and the Holy Spirit is a form of divination and is strictly forbidden by God (Lev. 19: 26; 2 Kings 17: 17–18; Acts 16: 16–18).

(3) **Magic/witchcraft/sorcery** which is the manipulation of evil spirits in order to obtain a result. Witches (female magicians), wizards (male magicians) and sorcerers, all use evil spirits to manipulate people and circumstances. Magic, witchcraft, and sorcery include practices like, *casting spells, incantations, enchantments, use of potions* and *charms, familiar spirits* (demons invited by a person to guide them) etc. No magic is good

magic, both black and white magic are forbidden (Ex. 22: 18; 1 Sam. 15: 23; Isa. 47: 9; Acts 8: 9–11; Gal. 5: 19–21).

(4) **New Age** practices

(5) Generally, all practices that place their faith in any thing other than God are wrong. For example faith in *objects*, *herbs*, *false prophets*, *people*, *demons*, and *idols* are all forbidden by God. The **occult**, *satanism*, *omens*, *signs*, and all *false religions* and *belief systems* are also forbidden by God (Deut. 18: 10–12).

Believers should not necessarily study all of these practices but should know *more or less* what they involve in order to avoid them and teach against them (2 Cor. 2: 11). There are always demonic spirits behind every one of these practices. Once the spirit behind the activity is identified, it can then be bound or cast out by the believer. See also **Deliverance; False Religion/Beliefs; Satan/Demons.**

Deliverance: This is the *removal*, *binding* or *casting out* of demonic spirits from operating in a person's body, soul or spirit. It may also be called **exorcism**. Deliverance can be done through the **prayer** of another believer or by the oppressed believer using the Word of God. To be delivered and live demon free is a right of every believer and nothing less should be accepted. The **deliverance ministry** is about bringing freedom to people who are controlled or oppressed by demonic spirits. Although all believers are called to live demon free and to exercise authority over demons, some believers have been given more grace by God than others to deliver people from demonic bondages and generational curses. These people are often referred to as **deliverance ministers**. Deliverance is done through the casting out of the devils or by binding their work and activity. Both of these ways are Biblical ways of dealing with demons (Mark 16: 17–18;

Luke 10: 19). See also **Demonic Strongholds; Demonic/Forbidden Practices; Generational Curses; Spiritual Warfare**

Demonic Oppression: This refers to the operation of demonic activity in a person's life causing different kinds of harassment. These can include mental attacks, illness, depression, lack, poverty, temptation, stagnation etc. (John 10: 10; Acts 5: 16; 10: 38; 1 Pet. 5: 8). When a person becomes indwelt and controlled by demonic spirits this is called **demonic possession.** At this stage the demon dwells within the spirit and soul if the person is a non-believer and within the soul only if the person is a believer. This is because the spirit of a believer cannot be possessed, as God dwells within it. (1 Cor. 2: 16; 6: 19). Believers have the **authority** and the **power** to be delivered from demonic oppression and possession in Jesus name. They also have the **authority** and **power** to cast out demons from others who are oppressed and possessed (Matt. 17: 14–18; Mark 5: 1–20; Acts 16: 16–18). See also **Deliverance; Satan/Demons; Spiritual Warfare.**

Demonic possession: See **Demonic Oppression.**

Demonic strongholds: See **Strongholds.**

Demons: See **satan/demons.**

Demonstrate the Kingdom of God: See **Kingdom of God.**

Demonstration of Power: See **Demonstrations of the Holy Spirit.**

Demonstrations of the Holy Spirit: This refers to the display, manifestation or exhibition of the power of God in the natural realm. It is also commonly called the **demonstration of power, kingdom demonstration, demonstrating the kingdom** etc. Demonstrations of the Holy Spirit include but are not limited to the **operations of the Holy Spirit, gifts of the Holy Spirit, signs, wonders,** and **miracles**. Every believer must be able to demonstrate God's Kingdom in one way or another (Matt. 16: 19; Mark 16: 17–20; Luke 10: 17, 19; 17: 21; John 14: 12; 1 Cor. 4: 20). See also **Authority; Kingdom of God; Power of God**

Descension Gifts: See **Gifts of the Spirit.**

Dimension: This refers to the *measure, level,* or *area* of **anointing,** gifts, or **grace** operating in the life of a believer. For example moving in the apostolic dimension would mean displaying the signs or gifts of the apostle. See also **Glory to Glory; Faith to Faith.**

Discerning of Spirits: refers to the gift of the Holy Spirit which reveals the type of spirits operating in a particular person, place or situation. These maybe angels, **demons,** or the Holy Spirit. This is not being perceptive or being a good judge of character because that comes from the natural mind. This gift instead, is revealed in the spiritual mind by God (2 Kings 6: 16–17; Acts 14: 7–10). See also **Prophetic gifts**

Discipling/Discipleship: See **Spiritual Mentoring**

Divination: See **Demonic/Forbidden Practices.**

Divine Nature: See **Born Again**

Divine Revelation: See **Revelation.**

Doctrine: A doctrine refers to a *set of beliefs, principles, instructions,* and *teachings*. It may also simply mean *that which is taught*. The doctrine of a believer therefore means the fundamental set of beliefs or principles that he or she believes in from the Bible regarding different areas of the Bible. Some believers will emphasize on certain doctrine or teachings more than others depending on the area of revelation they operate in the most. **Sound doctrine or teachings** refers to teachings and beliefs that have been rightly divided or correctly interpreted from the Bible and which are in line with what the Holy Spirit intended for them to mean in the context of other related Scriptures. The doctrine of a believer is usually shaped by the **ministers** that inspire him or her as they are driven by the **calling** on their lives. What is important is that all doctrine conforms to the overall truth of the Bible as the highest authority. Otherwise it is error or **false doctrine**. The doctrine of a believer also becomes important as they desire to go into ministry. A believer must be established in an overall belief system of what he or she believes is the truth from the many aspects of the Bible. It is not necessary to know all aspects just the most important. For example believers must at least have revelation of **salvation, healing, prosperity**, but may not necessarily have it on **eschatology**, levels of demonic operation, study of the different prophets, Greek and Hebrew translations etc. (Eph. 4: 14; 1 Tim. 1: 10; 2 Tim. 3: 16; Titus 1: 9). See also **Message.**

Dominion Movement: See **Dominion.**

Dominion: It is the word *radah* in the Hebrew, and it refers to the 'rule' and 'authority of royalty or a king'. It is used with the word 'subdue' in Genesis 1: 28, which is the word *kabash* in the Hebrew, which means 'to enslave'. It also means 'defeating a military enemy'. Dominion was lost at the **fall of man** or Adam but was restored back to believers in **Christ**. Believers therefore can and must walk in this dominion. **Dominionists** are believers who practice and preach Dominion as their central message. The **Dominion movement** is the numbers around the world that God is raising to preach and **activate** the message of dominion within believers. One of the central beliefs of dominion as a teaching is the reclaiming of the **Seven mountain kingdoms** (Gen. 1: 26–28; Ps. 8: 6; Rom. 5: 17; Col. 2: 15; 1 John 3: 8; 4: 17; Luke 10: 19). See also **Authority.**

Dominionists: See **Dominion**

Double-Portion Anointing: This refers to the type of empowerment or ability given by the Holy Spirit which multiplies, increases or accelerates the **anointing** operating in a believer's life. The prophet Elisha asked for and received this enablement through the prophet Elijah (2 Kings 2: 9–15). As a result of the double-portion anointing he has more recorded miracles in the Bible. Any believer can ask and receive this multiplication of the Holy Spirit's empowerment. Even though the anointing multiplied by double in the case of Elisha, there is room for more than double in the case of the New Testament believer in Christ (1 Kings 17; 2 Kings 13). See also **Activation; Impartation; Mantle.**

Drunk in the Spirit: See **New Wine.**

Dream: This refers to the communication given by God to a person through pictures (*stationary or moving*) and sometimes words while the person is asleep (Gen. 37: 5–9; Matt. 1: 18–25; Acts 2: 17). See also **Vision; Trance.**

Dunamis: See **Power of God.**

-E-

Edify/Edification: Edify in the Greek is *oikodome*, which means to 'build, erect, or put stones into place'. Edification is one of the functions of a prophetic message according to 1 Cor. 14: 3. When believers edify one another, they build up their spirit man and raise their faith levels by speaking words from God. Edification also has the ability to build God's purpose for a believer in the **spirit realm** because of its prophetic nature (Jer. 1:9–10). See also **Exhort/ Exhortation; Prophetic Gifts.**

Elder: This word comes from the Greek word *presbuteros* and refers to any person who has been placed in a position of oversight and leadership over others in a **local church**. This should come by virtue of their proven maturity in **character** and in the Word of God. Elders can therefore include, deacons, bishops, and **Five Fold Ministers** (Acts 14: 23, 20: 28; 1 Tim. 3: 1–13; 4: 14; 1 Pet. 5: 1–4, 5: 17; Titus 1: 5–9). See also **Bishop; Commission; Deacon.**

El-Elyon: See **Names of God.**

Elijah Company/Type of Prophets: See **Elijah Spirit.**

Spirit: This refers to an **anointing** that will enable believers to operate like Elijah with **authority** over kings, evil spirits, in miracles, and in the **prophetic ministry.** The Elijah spirit is based on scriptures like

Malachi 4: 5–6, and Mark 9: 12–13, which speak about Elijah coming before Jesus. As John the Baptist was a type of Elijah before Jesus came on the earth, even so there will be a people God will raise as a type of Elijah with the ability to operate like Elijah before the **Second Coming** of Jesus. The **Elijah company/type of prophets** refers to prophets that will operate as Elijah did. This teaching is amplified by the fact that Elijah left His mantle on the earth with Elisha, and even when Elisha died the mantle still produced miracles *(2* Kings 2: 9–13, 13: 21).

Elohim: See **Names of God.**

El-Olam: See **Names of God.**

El-Roi: See **Names of God.**

El-Shaddai: See **Names of God.**

End-Time Transfer of Wealth: This refers to the *exchanging or redistribution of money, materials, land, resources, and influence from the control and hands of the unsaved into the hands of the believers.* Popularly known as the **wealth transfer**, it may mean a *single transfer* as in Exodus 3: 19–22 and it can also refer to the *season* or a period prophesied and ordained by God in which this transfer will take place. The **faith** built around this concept centres on prophecies of scripture. The **Church** and believers are going to operate with **dominion** over the earth before the coming of Jesus and this wealth will be needed for the largest harvest of souls or **great harvest** prophesied in these days (Deut. 6: 10–12; Prov. 13: 22; Eccl. 2: 26; Isa. 60; Joel 2: 23–27). See also **Power to Prosper; Prosperity; Seven Mountain Kingdoms**

End-Time Harvest: This speaks about the final move of the Holy Spirit to bring many to **salvation**, in these last days. More souls will come than ever before to saving power of Jesus as we wait for His return (Joel 3: 14; Matt. 13: 38–39). See also **Power Evangelism; Winning Souls/Witnessing**

End Times refers to the close of the era of sin and satan on the earth. It refers to the time when God will establish His kingdom on the earth and judge the nations. This time is also known as the **Day of the Lord**, the **Last** or **Final hour/days**. Before Jesus does return it will be a time of **Great tribulation**. It will also be a time for the believer's greatest grace to move in the **spiritual gifts, dominion, power, and authority**. Most believers as well as **apostolic** and **prophetic pioneers** believe we are living in these times (Joel 2: 31; Luke 21: 10–33; 2 Pet. 3: 8–10; 1 John 2: 18). See also **Eschatology.**

Equipping: See **TEAR Programme.**

Error: See **Doctrine.**

Eschatology: This refers to the study and teachings of the **end times**. Such study often involves a close look at current world events like politics, natural disasters, state of the world etc. and compares them to the truths and prophecies of the Bible (Luke 21: 29–31). See also **New Jerusalem; Rapture; Second Coming.**

Evangelical Movement: See **Movement.**

Evangelist: This is one of the **Fivefold offices** mentioned in *Ephesians 4: 11*. This word is translated from the Greek word *euaggelizo*, which directly means 'a bringer of good news or good tidings'. Although all believers are called to evangelize or witness, evangelists are chosen and anointed by God especially for this reason. Evangelists have a unique ability to attract crowds and relate the gospel in such a manner that it convicts the hearts of the hearers enabling many souls to be won to Jesus Christ. The gifts, grace or anointing that follow the evangelist are usually **special faith** and **miracles** (Acts 21: 8; 2 Tim. 4: 5). See also **Power Evangelism/ Witnessing; Winning Souls;**

Exhort/Exhortation: This is one of the gifts of the Holy Spirit mentioned in Romans 12: 8. It is the **grace** given to a believer to encourage others. This word (exhort) in the Greek is *paraklesis*, which means to 'offer comfort or consolation'. Exhortation is one of the functions of a prophetic message according to 1 Cor. 14: 3. When a believer exhorts another, he or she boosts the person's spirit to walk in the truth of God concerning his or her life. Comforting is one of the key functions of the Holy Spirit. The word *Comforter,* referring to the Holy Spirit in John 14: 16, is the Greek word *parakletos*, which means 'someone that has been called to one's side to give aid and assistance'. Even though exhortation is a gift, all believers must exhort other believers. This is because exhortation encourages other believers to walk in that place where God wants them to be. Exhortation can give direction to a discouraged and directionless person. This is part of the commandment to **love** given to all of us by Jesus Christ according John 13: 34–35 and His prayer in John 17 (Acts 15: 31; Eph. 4: 29; 1 Tim. 4: 13; Heb. 3: 13; 10: 25). See also **Edify/Edification.**

Exorcism: See **Deliverance.**

Extremes: This refers to any aspect of truth from the Bible that has been overemphasised to the point of becoming **error** or **unsound doctrine. Extreme teachings** are unbalanced interpretations of the Bible that are taught to people. These are dangerous because they can lead people astray. That is why it is the responsibility of every believer to search out the scriptures for themselves (Acts 17: 10–11; Gal. 1: 6–9; 2 Tim. 2: 15). See also **Doctrine.**

Faith Confessions/Decrees/Declarations: This refer to speaking God's Word over a situation by faith. The Greek word for confession is *homolgeo*, which means 'saying the same thing God says and then agreeing with it'. It is also often called **speaking the Word**, or **speaking life**. Believers must regularly confess God's word over the areas in their lives in which they want to see God change and affect, just as God spoke things into existence (Gen. 1: 1–25). Even so, believers have been empowered to do the same. The Bible empowers the believer to speak things than do not exist as though they did, in order for them to materialise (Prov. 18: 21; Matt 12: 37; 15: 8; Rom. 4: 17; 10: 8; Heb. 4: 12). See also **Faith; Meditation; Prayer**

Faith Movement: See **Movement.**

Faith to Faith: See **Faith.**

Faith: Faith is to *believe with eager expectation that what God has said concerning us is true and will happen for us.* Faith is a necessary ingredient to receiving answered prayers and for manifesting any **spiritual gifts.** The lack or absence of faith is **unbelief.** The source of faith is God's Word. The term **faith to faith** refers to the increase in the faith level that operates within a believer (Rom. 1: 17). Faith is able to grow and increase as well as decrease. Every believer is called by God to ascend into new levels of faith in His Word. There are two main kinds of faith:

(1) General faith, which refers to the faith that, we all receive when we become **born again**. It comes as a seed and grows, according to the level of revelation we allow ourselves to receive from the Word of God. Faith can be placed both on the *rhema* and *logos*. It is therefore possible to have faith in the fulfilment of **personal prophecies, visions, dreams,** etc.

(2) **Special/supernatural faith** refers to the *quickening or the enhancing of a believer's level of faith in order for God to do a speedy work*. Special faith comes directly from God (1 Cor. 12: 9). God operates where there is faith, so He does sometimes increase the level of faith in a believer in order to accomplish something for them or through them. Special faith is usually accompanied by **miracles**. The opposite of faith is *fear and unbelief.* (Matt. 13: 58; Mark 11: 22–24; Heb. 11: 1,6). See also **Faith Confessions/Decrees/Declarations; Fear; Meditation; Supernatural Boldness.**

Faithfulness: This is one of the **fruit of the Spirit**. It comes from the Greek word *pistis*. It means 'to commit oneself to something or someone'. Someone who is faithful can be classified as *reliable, consistent, loyal, dedicated, dependable* and *trustworthy*. This is the nature of God and the expectation for all believers (Prov. 28: 20; 1 Cor. 10: 13; 1 Thess. 5: 24; 2 Tim. 2: 2). See also **Character.**

Faith-Healing Movement: See **Movement.**

Fall of Man/Adam: This refers to the first act of disobedience from mankind towards God, that happened in the Garden of Eden, through Adam and Eve. This fall, also called the **original sin** resulted in the following for all of mankind:

(1) Spiritual death or separation from God through our spirits. Mankind became disconnected and lost communion with the presence of God (Gen. 2: 17; Rom. 6: 23).

(2) Earth was cursed and all that is in it, resulting in labour and hard work for everything. This curse and separation from God brought sin, sickness, physical death, poverty, and lack (Gen. 3: 17–19).

(3) Man inherited the **sin-nature**, which made sin dominate him. Satan received authority to act on the earth and uses sin to drive mankind further from God. (Ps. 51: 5; Eph. 2: 3; 1 John 1: 8).

Jesus Christ came as the second Adam to reverse most of the effects of this fall of mankind (Rom. 5: 12–21). See also **Born Again; Sin.**

Falling under the Power: See **Slain in the Spirit.**

False Apostle: See **Apostle.**

False Doctrine: See **Doctrine.**

False Prophet: This is an individual who will give credibility to the **antichrist** and cause people to worship him. He is most likely to be a religious leader who is well respected by people, so he will be able to influence them (Rev 13: 11–18). See also **Eschatology.**

False Prophets: See **Prophet.**

False Religion/Beliefs: This refers to all religions and belief systems that deny or misinterpret some or all aspects of the Bible. Most of these false beliefs deny Jesus Christ in one or more of the following ways:

(1) That He is God.

(2) That He is fully man and fully God.

(3) That He is sinless.

(4) That He is the only source to God, heaven, and/or **salvation**.

These religions include but are not limited to Islam, Hinduism, Buddhism, Judaism, Atheism, Mormonism, Jehovah's Witnesses, Scientology, New Age beliefs, some practices of Roman Catholicism (e.g., worship of the Virgin Mary, praying through saints, etc.). The Bible is clear in that it alone is the only Truth and the very Word of God (John 1: 1–3; 17: 17; 2 Tim. 3: 16–17). It is also clear that Jesus Christ is fully God, and the only access available to God is through Him and His blood sacrifice on the cross. All other beliefs that are in any manner inconsistent with this view stem from man and satan. Any attempt to place any faith or hope in an object, person, or other god is a false religion (Isa. 9: 6; John 1: 1–3; 8: 57–59; Col. 2: 9; Heb. 1: 8). See also **Antichrist; Demonic/Forbidden Practices; Doctrine.**

False/Lying Signs and Wonders: This refers to signs, wonders, miracles, healings or any acts of the **supernatural** that are performed by humans through the power of demonic spirits. The purpose of these lying supernatural acts is to deceive people and to remove them from focusing on Jesus Christ and His word. The Bible warns that believers need to ensure that the source of all supernatural activities come from God. This can be done by **testing the spirits** which involves mainly two aspects:

(1) Comparing the person's teaching and practices against the *Bible* and,

(2) Relying on the *Holy Spirit* for **revelation** through the gift of **discerning of spirits** (Matt. 24: 24; Rev. 16: 13–14). See also

Demonic/Forbidden Practices; False Apostles; Signs and Wonders.

Familiar with the Anointing/Mantle: In a *positive* sense it refers to a situation where believers have become acquainted with the gifts and **calling** of another believer, such as to build a relationship of trust and confidence in the man or woman of God. In a *negative* sense it refers to a situation where believers have become acquainted with the gifts and calling of another believer, such as to become complacent, and no longer approach the **anointing** or **mantle** with and expectation and **faith** or that the anointing or mantle will impact or affect their lives in a positive way. Believers usually develop this lazy approach to a mantle and anointing of a leader they see and hear regularly. The opposite of this approach is for believers to always keep on **placing a demand on the mantle/anointing** of a man or woman of God in faith and expectation that what they are carrying, God will use to bless and increase their lives. See also **Honouring Leaders; Prophet's Reward.**

Fasting: This commonly refers to the abstinence from food and or drink in order to obtain a spiritual result. Fasting is a powerful way to access the **spiritual realm** in order to receive answers from God. Fasting involves the believer depriving the flesh of what it desires the most (food and drink) in order to allow their spirit to receive results from God. Believers should fast regularly as a discipline in order to maintain a strong spiritual life and be more sensitive and **receptive to the Holy Spirit**. (Ezra 8: 21; Est. 4: 16; Jon. 3: 5–10; Matt. 6: 18; Acts 13: 3, 14: 23; 1 Cor. 9: 27). See also **Spiritual Maturity.**

Fatherhood: This refers mainly to two aspects. The revelation of the Father of our Lord Jesus Christ being *accepted* and *appropriated* by believers in order to walk in the fullness as His sons and daughters.

This relates to the *identity* of believers as sons and daughters of a loving Father. Believers must move beyond the revelation of **salvation** only and enter into the benefits of walking as sons and daughters of their Father. God is more than Saviour and King; He is also our Father and our Daddy (John 20: 17; Rom. 8: 15; 2 Cor. 6: 18; Gal. 3: 26; 1 John 3: 1).

(2) It also speaks about the type of leaders that God is raising in these days over His people. These leaders invest their lives as fathers would do to their own children. This type of leadership style is called **fathering**. True **apostles** and **prophets** will bring about this selfless approach to leadership. **Fathers in the faith** (can also include mothers) refers to man or woman of that God has used in the past and present that have become a mentor and a role-model for others to follow (1 Cor. 4: 14–15; 11: 1). See also **Sons of God; Spiritual Parents: Spiritual Mentoring.**

Fathering: See **Fatherhood.**

Favour: See **Grace**

Fathers and Mothers in the Faith: See **Fatherhood.**

Fear: Webster's Dictionary defines fear as 'a feeling of anxiety and agitation produced by the presence or nearness of danger, evil, pain'. This is the opposite of **faith**. Fear should not be tolerated by believers because of the following reasons:

(1) It is forbidden by God. The Bible mentions the word *fear-not* and *do not fear* at-least 100 times (Deut. 31: 6; Josh. 1: 9).
(2) God is restricted to release His promises where fear is present. This is because only faith pleases God (Matt. 14: 26–31; Luke 8: 49–55; Heb. 11: 6).

(3) Believers have nothing to fear because God is on their side, and nothing can defeat of override the Word of God (Ps. 23: 4; Isa. 43: 1–2; 54: 17; Rom. 8: 38–39).

(4) Fear can allow **demonic doorways**, and permit satan and his demons to operate in a believer's life. This is because fear is from the devil. Fear is not a *mental force*, it is a *spiritual force* (2 Tim. 1: 7). God is able to deliver a believer from all fears when they are taken to Him in faith (Ps. 34: 4; 1 Pet. 5: 7). See also **Deliverance; Demonic Oppression.**

Fear and Trembling: See **Fear of the Lord/God.**

Fear of the Lord/God: Fear and trembling are two attributes the Bible encourages believers to have according to Phil. 2: 12. These actually mean believers are to reverence and respect God more than being terrified or afraid of Him. This is godly fear and reverence (Heb. 12: 28). Believers must live with the fear of God. Webster's Dictionary defines **fear** as 'a feeling of anxiety and agitation produced by the presence or nearness of danger, evil, or pain', but this fear of God does not involve an uneasy feeling of punishment, or danger, instead it is a love from within us to value and hold God in the high regard that He deserves. Fearing God and loving Him are therefore one and the same thing. This fear is the only fear believers are allowed to have, because it is not demonic in nature but comes from the Holy Spirit (Prov. 1: 7; Isa. 11: 1–2; Heb. 12: 28–29). See also **Holiness; Repentance**

Feeler/Knower: See **Prophet.**

Final Hours/Days: See **End Times.**

Final Wave: See **Third Day.**

Financing the Kingdom of God: See **Kings.**

Finishing Generation: See **Omega Generation.**

First Fruits: This refers to the first of whatever income that comes to a believer that is given back to God as an act of devotion, reverence and thanksgiving. This is usually done in the **local church**. It can be the first salary of a new job, the first increase, first profit of a new business etc. Giving God the first fruits is a form of worship and acknowledging that God is the source of whatever increase we get. (Ezek. 44: 30; Prov. 3: 9) *See* also **Offering; Sowing and Reaping; Tithe**

Fivefold Ministers/Offices: See **Fivefold Ministry.**

Fivefold Ministry: This refers to the gifts or positions given to the **Church** by Jesus Christ. The Fivefold ministry is an extension of the ministry of Jesus. This ministry consists of the **apostle, prophet, evangelist, pastor** and **teacher** according to Eph. 4: 11. They can sometimes be called **Fivefold ministers, offices,** or positions. These ministries were given by Jesus when He ascended into heaven, therefore they are also called the **ascension gifts**. *Not every believer is called into these offices.* These offices cannot be imparted from one believer to another because they are given directly by Jesus from before birth. They have the function of equipping believers to work in their membership ministries, in order to build the Body of Christ. This function includes removing the divisions among believers by bringing unity and by establishing scriptural truths, **doctrines,** and by exposing what is false (Eph. 4: 12–16). See also **Kings and Priests; Seven Mountain Kingdoms.**

Fornication: See **Sexual Immorality.**

Foundation of the Apostles and Prophets: See **Apostolic and Prophetic Leadership.**

Fresh Anointing: This refers to the *renewal* or *revival* of a gift or grace that has become inactive or is active but in a smaller proportion than it usually manifests. It can also refer to a new gift altogether. A fresh anointing usually comes with a stronger or greater passion for that gift to function. It can also be called a **fresh fire, fresh wind, fresh oil** because fire, wind, and oil are symbolic of the Holy Spirit and His Anointing (Ex. 30: 25–26; 1 Sam. 16: 13; Acts 19: 11–12). See also **Anointing; Gifts of the Holy Spirit; Operation of the Holy Spirit; Revival.**

Fresh Anointing: See **Anointing.**

Fresh Fire: See **Anointing.**

Fresh Wind: See **Anointing.**

Fruit of the Spirit: This refers to the attributes or character of the Holy Spirit or God seen or evidenced through a believer. The word *fruit* means *that which is inward and comes out*. Fruit of the Spirit can also refer to the **character** of a believer. Generally the growth of a believer is seen in the Fruit of the Spirit more than in the **gifts of the Holy Spirit**. The fruit is listed in Gal. 5: 22–23 as **love, joy, peace, patience, kindness, goodness, faithfulness, gentleness** (meekness), and **self-control** (self-discipline), but the fruit of the Spirit can also include holiness, righteousness, **praise and worship**, thanksgiving, etc. (1 Cor. 6: 19; Col. 3: 12–16; Phil. 4: 4; Heb. 12: 14). See also **Yielding to the Holy Spirit.**

General Will of God: See **Calling**

Generational Curses: This refers to curses and demonic operations that have been passed on from parents to their children, grand-children, great grandchildren etc. These curses occur because of reasons such as sin, **demonic or forbidden practices**, involvement in the **occult** and **witchcraft**. Generational curses do not leave simply because a person has received Jesus as Lord and Saviour. These curses can often be detected where there is a *trend, pattern, or similarities with generations from the same blood line*, a trend in *behaviour* (violence, anger, lust, abuse, etc.), a trend in *addictions* (drugs, alcohol, etc.), or a trend in *circumstances* (easy job loss, disfavour, extramarital pregnancy, divorce, imprisonment, etc.). Put in another way, generational curses can be identified where there are common problems or difficulties. This is one of the areas that believers need to be free from after they have received Jesus as Lord. Breaking these curses is one of the reasons for which He came to the earth according to 1 John 3: 8. Believers must also exercise their authority and pray over others who have generational curses (Ex. 34: 7; Lam. 5: 7; Gal. 3: 13). See also **Deliverance; Demonic Oppression; Satan/Demons.**

Gentleness/Meekness: This is one of the **fruit of the Spirit.** It comes from the Greek word *prautes*. It has the following meanings: mild of temper, soft, gentle, submissive to divine will and to others, to be yielding, lowliness, humble, not-proud (Gal. 6: 1; Eph. 4: 2; 2 Tim. 2: 24; 1 Pet. 3: 15). See also **Character; Submitting to Spiritual Authority.**

Gift of Compassion/Mercy: See **Compassion/Mercy.**

Gift of Giving: See **Giving.**

Gift of Healing: See **Healing.**

Gift of Interpretation of Tongues: See **Interpretation of Tongues.**

Gift of Leadership: See **Leadership.**

Gift of Ministry: See **Ministry.**

Gift of Miracles: See **Miracles.**

Gift of Prophecy: See **Prophecy.**

Gift of Teaching: See **Teaching.**

Gift of Tongues: This is a gift of the Holy Spirit which covers two main aspects: (1) The enablement given to a believer to speak in a *spiritual language* as the words are given by the Holy Spirit. (2) The enablement given to a believer to speak in a *natural language* that they cannot naturally speak in. For example an English speaking person speaking Spanish or French even though they do not ordinarily know how to. Every believer should be able to speak in the *spiritual language*, because it is a free and a very important gift. (Acts 2: 1–21; 1 Cor. 12: 10; 14: 21–22). See also **Gifts of the Spirit.**

Gifts of the Spirit: These are supernatural abilities given to believers by the Holy Spirit. They are also called **Spiritual gifts**. There are at least twenty-eight spiritual gifts that can be identified in the Bible. Gifts of the Spirit are **supernatural** and have nothing to do with human strengths, capabilities, or talents.

There are three broad categories of Spiritual gifts mentioned in 1 Cor. 12: 8–10, which are

(1) **Power gifts:** Working of **miracles, special faith,** gifts of **healing.** They are called power gifts because they demonstrate the power of the Holy Spirit.

(2) **Utterance gifts: Tongues, Prophecy, Interpretation of tongues.** They are called utterance gifts because they are uttered or spoken.

(3) **Revelation gifts: Word of knowledge, word of wisdom** and **discerning of spirits.** They are called revelation gifts because they come by **revelation** of the Holy-Spirit.

Gifts of the Holy Spirit that came with the Holy Spirit being sent to earth are called **descension gifts,** while **ascension gifts** refer to the **Fivefold ministry. Talents** can often be confused with spiritual gifts, but they are not. This is because most talents proceed from the *natural* human being, whether the person is a believer in Jesus Christ or not. However spiritual gifts are only available to born-again believers. Believers have an advantage in that, the talents, strengths or abilities that come naturally to them can be enhanced to function supernaturally or above their natural limits by the Holy Spirit (Rom. 12: 6–8; 1 Cor. 12: 8–10; Eph. 4: 11). See also **Anointing; Fivefold Ministry; Grace.**

Giving: It is one of the gifts of the Holy Spirit mentioned in Rom. 12: 8, therefore it is also called the **gift of giving.** It is an enablement given by the Holy Spirit to a believer to *give* or *support* God and His people in *finances* and *resources*; however, all believers are called to be givers according to the Bible (Prov. 19: 17; Luke 6: 38; 2 Cor. 9: 7). The Holy Spirit has given other believers more grace to move in this gift than others. Giving can progress to the next level or to a larger scale where the believer finances the Kingdom of God. This gift in these last days will be seen through the establishment of Kingdom Banks and **God-owned companies** and **businesses**. *See* also **Kings; Prosperity.**

Glory Dimension: See **Glory.**

Glory to Glory: See **Glory.**

God Makes the Man before the Ministry: See **Character.**

God: See **Godhead/Trinity.**

Glory: In the Hebrew it is the word *kabod*, meaning 'weight' or 'heaviness'. It also means 'honour', 'importance', and 'majesty'. In the Greek it is the word *doxa*, which means 'brightness'. The glory of God speaks about God revealing His *essence, presence, power, majesty,* or His beauty to be seen, felt and heard and not only sensed. The Glory may also speak about a certain **dimension** or level where God's presence can be witnessed or sensed. This sort of atmosphere is often referred to as **open heaven**. When the glory of God is manifested signs such as silver and gold dust, angels, angel feathers, heavenly manna, smoke, clouds, oil, creative miracles etc. can be seen. The **Shekinah glory** refers to the visible presence of God's glory which is usually seen in a cloud of smoke (Ex. 16: 7; Isa. 40: 5; Hab. 2: 14). Going from **glory to glory** refers to the increase of the glory **dimension** operating or present in the life of a believer. Every believer is called by God to ascend into new levels of glory (2 Cor. 3: 18).

God's Timing: This refers to the set time, seasons and place in which God wants to do something through someone on the earth. The time taken to hear from God concerning His timing for a particular decision or answer is called **waiting on God/the Lord**. (Ps. 37: 7; Isa. 40: 31; Hab. 2: 3*)*. God's timing often goes with **God's release,** which is the *peace, comfort, or leading of the Holy Spirit* indicating that it is time for a believer to move in a certain direction or make certain decisions. God's timing and His release are needed most by believers when making big decisions like starting a church or a business, relocating countries, marriage etc. God's timing and His release lead to **open doors** and His **grace** (1 Sam. 30: 6–8; Ps. 27: 14; Eccl. 3: 11 Hab. 2: 3; Gal. 4: 4). See also **Longsuffering/Patience.**

Godhead/Trinity: God is three persons in one, or One Person who reveals Himself in three ways. (It is not three Gods but one). When God speaks about Himself, He uses the word 'us' in the Bible in Gen. 1: 26 and 11: 7–8. He is God the Father (Phil. 1: 2), God the Son (John 1: 1,14), and God the Holy Spirit (Acts 5: 3–4). This trio is called the Godhead, or the Trinity. The word trinity does not actually appear in the English translation (Rom. 1: 20; Col. 2: 9). It is easy to understand this when we consider humans are also three part beings; we are a spirit with a soul and live in a physical body (1 Thess. 5: 23). We are created in the very image of God and this is why we resemble Him as one in three (Gen. 1: 26 1 John 5: 7).

Here are some facts about the Godhead:

(1) The Father, Son and Holy Spirit are *equal in nature and character.*

(2) The Father Son and Holy Spirit are *always in agreement*; they function in *perfect harmony*. They can never contradict

one another; they move in *perfect union and synergy*. One cannot get jealous over the other because it is the same person revealed in three different ways.

(3) The Father, Son, and Holy Spirit can never fight within themselves because they have the *same heart and mind*.

(4) The Father, Son, and Holy Spirit are separate in personalities, but they are *all unique individuals*. Each of the Godhead has different roles to fulfil in the universe and in the believer's life. It is therefore important to receive revelation of each of them (2 Cor. 13: 14). The Father can be likened as the heart and mind of the Godhead, Jesus as the mouth, or Word, and the Holy Spirit as the hands or creative power of God. He is the one who creates things and brings them into the natural (Gen. 1; Mic. 2: 7).

Another way to look at the way they work is to say that the Father has the plans, Jesus will speak them, and the Holy Spirit will bring them into the natural. See also **Omni-Attributes of God.**

God/Word Consciousness: See **Demon/Devil Consciousness**

Goodness: This is one of the **fruit of the Spirit.** It comes from the Greek word *agathosune,* which means the state or quality of being good, character seen in quality or conduct, or the best part of anything (Rom. 11: 22; Eph. 5: 9). See also **Character; Kindness.**

Government of God: See **Kingdom of God.**

Grace: This is the willingness and **power of God** to accomplish something for or through a believer that cannot be done by human effort. It is God doing for us what we cannot do for ourselves because He loves us. Grace is first received at **salvation,** but grows and develops to bring the fullness of God's blessings and character within us. When grace manifests it makes things that are usually hard to become easy. Grace can also show itself in the **gifts of the Holy Spirit** or in the **anointing** on the life of a believer. All ministries and gifts must be operated by depending or leaning on His grace. The thesaurus meaning of grace and favour includes *excessive kindness, preferential treatment, unmerited favour, ease, goodwill, influence of God, to honour, kind act, unfair partiality, kind regard, to prefer, to aid or support, to approve.* Grace is given because of the finished work of Jesus Christ and not by our works. This is why it is called **unmerited** or undeserved **favour.**

The opposite of grace is **the law,** which covers at least two aspects:

(1) Following or observing the laws given to the Israelites by God in the Old Testament, which New Testament believers must not follow, unless the New Testament allows for it.

(2) It can also mean any self-imposed requirements, laws, rules, behaviour, rituals, and demands etc. that a believer places on their lives in an attempt to please God and receive His blessings. Everything God does for and through a believer is by His grace, and this is why He gets all the glory. (John 1: 17; Rom. 3: 24; 5: 2; 20–21; 2 Cor. 12: 9 Eph. 2: 8–10; 2 Pet. 3: 18). See also **Anointing; Gifts of the Spirit; Religious Spirit.**

Great Commission: See **Commission.**

Great Tribulation: This refers to a time on the earth where there will be much war, unrest and chaos especially towards the **Second Coming** of Jesus Christ (Matt. 24: 15–22; Mark 13: 14–24). See also **Eschatology; Rapture.**

-H-

Hallelujah: This is a word used to express **praise and worship** to God. It means 'praise the Lord'. It is a combination of two Hebrew words: *Hallel*, which means 'to praise, to boast in, to shine forth, to be worthy of praise, and to be commended'. *Jah* is a shortened form of *Jehovah*, which means 'the Self-Existent' and 'Eternal One'. This word is a rich meaning of praise and adoration to God and should be used regularly by believers to acknowledge God for His unending love and grace towards us. *See* also **Praise and Worship; Seeking the Face/Heart of God.**

Healing: This word is derived from the word *raphe* in the Hebrew, and ordinarily means 'to cure, cause to heal, repair, and make whole'. However, healing in the Bible can refer to curing a disease or wound and restoring it back to soundness, or to its natural functions (Matt. 14: 14; 20: 34). It can also mean restoring purity to a situation (2 Kings 2: 21–22; 2 Chron. 7: 14). This happens by God removing differences or sin in order to reconcile us to Him, this aspect can mean healing a breach or difference (Hos. 14: 4).

This type of healing, where God heals our sin, usually involves restoration to a place of prosperity. Healing through a believer is seen through the **gift of healing** given by the Holy Spirit which involves the supernatural intervention of God to a physical body to remove, cure or subdue a sickness or disease and to restore the body to its original healthy condition (1 Cor. 12: 9).

The Bible reveals that there is no limit to what God can cure through a believer. (HIV, cancer, heart disease, broken bones, and more can all be healed by faith in His Word). Healing often operates with signs such as **miracles, deliverance,** and **special faith** (Acts 5: 16, 10: 38). Healing also covers healing of the mind, heart, and emotions. The healing of the Lord can cure fears, depression, anxiety, suicide etc. (Rom. 12: 2; Phil. 4: 6–8; 1 Pet. 5: 7). See also **Inner Healing.**

Hearer: See **Prophet.**

Heavenly Hosts: See **Angelic Ministry.**

Heirs/Joint Heirs in Christ: See **Sons of God.**

Holiness: This is the state and nature of God and the **born-again** spirit of a believer. **Pursuing holiness** refers to the intentional actions and decisions taken by a believer to follow all that pleases God and separate himself or herself from all that displeases God.

There are two main words that describe the holy state of a believer in the Bible.

(1) **Justification** comes from *dikaiosi* in the Greek and means 'to declare righteous'. This is the *immediate* acquittal of a believer from all sin, guilt or condemnation by God through Jesus and His sacrifice on the cross (Rom. 4: 25; 5: 18).

(2) **Sanctification** comes from *hagiasmos* in the Greek and means 'to make holy'. This is a *continual* work within a believer to develop Christ likeness. Both justification and sanctification are necessary for holiness before God (Rom. 12: 1–2; 1 Cor. 6: 19–20; 1 Pet. 1: 13–16; 2 Pet. 3: 11–14). See also **Fear of the Lord/God**; **Righteousness.**

Holiness Movement: See **Movement**.

Holy Communion: Holy Communion refers to the connection a believer makes to Jesus Christ with the two elements that represent His blood (wine or grape juice) and His physical body (bread). The significance of this is to bring to remembrance the sacrifice and the finished work of Jesus Christ. Taking communion is both an act of worship and also a declaration of victory for the believer. It can therefore be taken as many times as possible as long as it is done in faith and not in a religious or ritualistic manner (Luke 22: 19–20; John 6: 53–56; 1 Cor. 11: 24–26). See also **Body of Christ.**

Holy Laughter: See **New Wine**.

Honouring Leaders: This refers to the tribute, respect, and acknowledgement shown to a leader or leaders in the **Body of Christ**. This can be a personal leader in the **local church**, or a general leader in the **fivefold ministry** or **seven mountain kingdoms**. It can also be referred to as **honouring spiritual fathers or mothers in the faith, honouring men or women of God** etc. This honour can be expressed through words, sowing, serving, submission, etc. (Gal. 6: 6; 1 Thess. 5: 12–13; 1 Tim. 5: 17–19; Heb. 13: 7). See also **Prophet's Reward; Spiritual Authority.**

Honouring Men/Women of God: See **Honouring Leaders**.

Honouring Spiritual Fathers and Mothers in the Faith: See **Honouring Leaders**.

Honouring the Mantle/Anointing: See **Mantle**.

I am That I am: See **Names of God.**

Identifying Gifts and Callings: This refers to the recognition and classification of the gifts of the Holy Spirit and the areas of callings that God has entrusted or given to a believer in order to enable them to function in their **membership role** in the Church and generally to be used by God. These gifts and callings are identified by using the **prophetic gifts** and observing the fruit and works in the life of a believer. **Apostolic and prophetic** leaders are very necessary for this process. *See* also **Calling; Gifts of the Holy Spirit; Prophetic Presbytery; TEAR Programme.**

Idolatry: This refers to the worship of any other thing, person or god other than the Father, Son, and Holy Spirit. Worship can also be any manner in which *excessive devotion* is given to any a person or an object. Idolatry can include but is not limited to the worship of images or gods through **false religions.** Believers must be careful to give their highest form of love and devotion only to God, and not money, material possessions, family, their job or career etc. The Bible connects the sin of **covetousness** to idolatry. Covetousness can be defined as the desire to have or possess something at any cost (Matt. 6: 24; Eph. 5: 5; Phil. 3: 19; Col. 3: 5). See also **God; Works/Sins/ Lusts of the Flesh.**

Impartation: This refers to the act of *transferring* anointing, gifts or grace from one person to another. While **activation** is done *within* a believer, impartation is deposited from *one believer to another*. Activation usually refers to a *non-active gift* while impartation usually refers to a *new gift* altogether. Impartation can come in some of the following ways:

(1) Attending a service or conference where the gift is practiced (1 Sam. 10: 6–13).

(2) By listening or reading material or receiving prayer or **laying on of hands** of a believer who moves in that gift.

(3) It can also come through **partnering** financially, sowing material things or by serving and associating with ministries that operate in a certain anointing, gifts or grace. The latter is called **anointing by association** (Matt. 10: 41; Rom. 1: 11; Gal. 6: 6–9; 2 Tim. 1: 6). See also **Calling; Gifts of the Spirit; Sowing into Anointing.**

Inner Healing: This refers to the process by which a believer receives healing from emotional and mental bondages or sickness. Inner-healing is needed often if a believer has kept within their heart and mind matters such as, **unforgiveness, fear,** bitterness, envy, strife, or pride. These sins can also be referred to as **sins of the heart.** These often come when a person has been hurt, abused or rejected in some way. Inner-healing also involves the restoration of a believer to *think the thoughts of God* for themselves and towards others. It is dangerous for believers to hold on to the sins of the heart as this can provide satan with a **legal right** or a foothold in a person's life. This can lead to greater sin, **demonic bondages,** sickness and even loss of their salvation. Legal rights refer to anything that can give demons permission to operate in the life of a believer. Jesus can take away any past hurt or shame if we give it to Him and choose to let go of it (Ps. 147: 3; Matt. 11: 28–30; Luke 4: 18; Rom. 12: 2; 1 Pet. 5: 7).

Intercession: This refers to the prayers of a believer or a group of believers offered on behalf of other people. Intercession can include with it **fasting.** Intercession can also be offered by praying in the **gift of tongues** (Rom. 8: 26). Intercession is also called **standing in the gap.** (Ezek. 22: 30). God needs intercessors to pray for the following:

(1) **For the lost,** which are the unsaved and backslidden.

(2) Governments and rulers to be saved and obey the Word of God (1 Tim. 2: 1–3).

(3) Church leaders, the Church and believers in general to be in the perfect will of God. This includes to be strengthened, protected, provided for, etc. (Eph. 6: 18; 1 Thess. 5: 25; James 5: 16).

(4) Prayers to oppose the **kingdom of darkness** and establish the **kingdom of God** on earth. Intercession is a necessary and powerful tool for God to use in order to advance His Kingdom. All believers must therefore pray for others, and more especially those who sense a calling for intercession. Some forms of intercession include **prayer walks** where believers walk to a particular place and intercede (Josh. 1: 3). And **prayer watches** where usually a group of believers pray for a long period of time, often in shifts or rotations. (Eph. 6: 18; 1 Thess. 1: 2; 1 Tim. 2: 1).

Interpretation of tongues: This is a gift of the Holy Spirit which allows a believer to interpret the meaning of a message spoken in tongues. The tongues to be interpreted can be spoken either by the same believer or another believer. Interpretation of tongues is not translation or transliteration, meaning one sentence in the natural language can be many sentences spoken in tongues or vice-versa. Speaking in tongues and interpreting them will result in a believer understanding the will of God, as it allows a believer to listen in on what they are praying for. This is because the Holy Spirit always prays the perfect will of the Father (Rom. 8: 26–27). Interpretation of tongues is a good way to practice listening to the voice of God and for moving in the prophetic ministry. A believer must learn to regularly listen in on what the Spirit of God is saying in his or her private prayer time, and then write it down. Usually interpretation will come by the person *knowing*, or *sensing*, or *thinking* the interpreted meaning. However the interpretation can also come through the several other ways in which God speaks (1 Cor. 2: 9–14, 12: 10) *See* also **Journaling; Practicing the Presence of God.**

-J-

Jezebel Spirit: This refers to a certain type of demonic spirit or influence. This spirit is identified according to the characteristics of the woman Jezebel in the Bible. The Bible does not speak about a *Jezebel spirit* but about Jezebel's conduct and character. This spirit is usually identified by the following characteristics:

(1) Opposing God's true worship and prophetic voice.
(2) Manipulating high ranking officials to oppose the Gospel of Jesus Christ.
(3) Manipulative, controlling and selfish behaviours.
(4) **Sexual immorality**.
(5) **Idolatry** (Generally read 1 & 2 Kings; Rev. 2: 18–29).

Jehovah/Yahweh: See **Names of God**.

Jehohav-Nissi: See **Names of God**.

Jehovah-Jireh: See **Names of God**.

Jehovah-Maccaddeshem: See **Names of God**.

Jehovah-Rapha: See **Names of God**.

Jehovah-Rohi: See **Names of God**.

Jehovah-Sabbaoth: See **Names of God.**

Jehovah-Shalom: See **Names of God.**

Jehovah-Shamah: See **Names of God.**

Jehovah-Tsidkenu: See **Names of God.**

Joshua Assignment/Mandate: See **Joshua Generation.**

Joshua Generation: This refers to a generation that will follow in the mandate God gave to Joshua which is known as the **Joshua assignment** or **mandate**. This mandate includes taking the land and wealth God has promised His people and destroying His and our enemies. The Joshua generation is characterized as being passionate, uncompromising and ready to take the Promised Land. Although the Promised Land literally referred to Israel for the Jewish people, for the Church it speaks about the whole earth which is our inheritance (Deut. 7: 1–2; Josh. 1: 1–5, 21: 43–45, 24: 14–15).

Journaling: This refers to the process of writing down, anything that relates to God and the life of a believer, especially in a book or journal dedicated for that purpose. It can include writing down thoughts, ideas, psalms, poems, letters, etc. Believers must regularly use this method as a way of growing in hearing the voice of God for themselves and for others (Ps. 119: 105; Hab. 2: 2). See also **Practicing the Presence of God; Prophetic Gifts;** *Rhema.*

Joy: This is one of the **fruit of the Spirit,** and it comes from the Greek word *chara*, which means 'to be cheerful, gladness of heart, calmly delightful'. The source of the believer's joy is not based on events or happenings (where we get the word happiness). Instead it comes from

God. This is why the Bible calls it the joy of the Lord and the joy of the Holy Spirit. (Neh. 8: 10; 1 Thess. 1: 6). The Bible commands the believer to maintain an attitude of joy and thanksgiving. This is because rejoicing is based on God's unfailing goodness and it releases **faith** to rise up within the believer (Phil. 4: 4; 1 Thess. 5: 16, 18). See also **Character.**

Judgement of Believers: See **Judgement of God.**

Judgement of God: The Bible speaks mainly of two kinds of judgement that will take place after we die. The **Great White Throne Judgement**, which is where Jesus will judge the living and the dead, both sinners and believers. At this judgement He will open up the Book of Life to see the names contained within it and all those whose names are not found in the Book of Life will be cast into the lake of fire forever (Rev. 2011–15).

The ones that are found in the Book of Life will proceed to the judgement of believers. This is where all believers will come before the **Judgement seat of Christ,** which is set up for judgement. The **Judgement of believers** will evaluate every believer's works according to the will of God and then reward us accordingly (Rom. 14: 10–12; 2 Cor. 5: 10; Heb. 9: 27).

Judgement Seat of Christ: See **Judgement of God**

Justification: See **Holiness.**

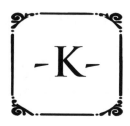

Kindness: This is one of the **fruit of the Spirit.** It comes from the Greek word *chrestotes*, which means 'the ability to act for the good or betterment of those who oppose your patience or try you'. Kindness is seen mainly in actions. Paul uses this fruit as one of the indications of being a commendable minister of God in *2* Cor. 6: 4–6 (Rom. 11: 22; 2 Pet. 1: 7) See also **Character; Goodness.**

Kingdom Building: This refers to any manner in which the Kingdom of God is advanced. Since the **Kingdom of God** governs so many areas, even so kingdom building includes any way in which the rule or government of God is seen on the earth.

Kingdom Now Movement: See **Kingdom of God.**

Kingdom Now: See **Kingdom of God.**

Kingdom Owned Businesses: This refers to businesses, companies or any projects that generate wealth for God and His gospel. These type of entities have God as the main shareholder and all or most of the profits go wherever He leads or guides the believer. God is raising more and more of this model of business as one of the tools for taking the wealth of the sinners and placing it in the hands of believers. *See* also **End-Time Transfer of Wealth; Financing the Kingdom; Kings; Power to Prosper**

Kingdom of God: Kingdom is the Greek word *basileia*, which means 'royal power, kingship, dominion', or the 'right or authority to rule over another kingdom'. This term therefore refers to the rule or government of God on the earth seen through the believers' kingship, power, dominion, right or **authority** given to them by the King of kings. This kingdom can refer to two areas: (1) Anyplace God establishes His order and His way of doing things (in other words anywhere His rule or dominion is physically seen in any of the **seven mountain kingdoms)**. (2) The kingdom can also refer to a place in the **spiritual realm** where believers function from, since we are already seated with Christ in heavenly places according to Eph. 2: 6. To **demonstrate the kingdom of God** means to display or manifest the Word of God on the earth through a believer's faith. This can be signs and wonders, healing, finances, deliverance etc. **Kingdom now** refers to establishing this government now before Jesus physically brings it in its fullness on the earth. **Kingdom now** and **kingdom of God movement** have been birthed from this principle (Dan. 4: 3; Matt. 3: 2; Luke 16: 16). See also **New Jerusalem.**

Kingdom of Darkness: This refers to the rule or government of **satan** and his **demons**, which opposes the **Kingdom of God**. This kingdom operates by influencing people to disobey God and His Word. Believers have been taken out of this kingdom and have been given **power** and **authority** over it (Luke 10: 19; Acts 26: 18; Eph. 6: 12; Col. 1: 13; 2: 15). See also **Deliverance; Demonic/Forbidden Practices; False Religions/Beliefs; Spiritual Warfare; Strongholds.**

Kingdom of God Movement: See **Kingdom of God.**

Kingly Believer: This refers to a believer who has the gifts, anointing or grace of a king, but does not necessarily function as a king full time. An example may be a full time **pastor** who manages his or her own business but focuses most of their attention on the **local church.** See also **Kings; Seven Mountain Kingdoms.**

Kings and priests: This term by the *logos* definition, refers to the state or nature of every believer given to us by Jesus as our King of kings and our High Priest. This is why the Bible calls believers royal priesthood. (1 Pet. 2:9) This king or priest position applies to both male and female. By the *rhema* meaning it refers to two categories of believers. (1) Kings are 'market' or 'secular world' based. They are believers that God has anointed to penetrate, influence and dominate the seven major areas of human life and activity (government, education, economy, family, media, religion, and arts) These believers are ministers of God just as preachers are. They are fully empowered and recognized by God. Joseph, Daniel & Esther in the Bible are examples of this type of believer. (2) The priests are mainly church based. They are believers who have been called into the fivefold offices, (**apostles, prophets, evangelists, pastors** and **teachers**) as well as believers who serve in the local church full time without necessarily being a Fivefold minister. (Rev. 1:6; 5:10; Heb. 2:17; 4:14). The **Kings and Priests Movement** is a movement dedicated to identifying, maturing and sending those called as kings and priests, in order to establish the government of God. A combination of fivefold offices plus seven areas to dominate equals the number twelve, which is the number representing the government of God. This movement when it is in full operation will usher in the **rapture** and ultimately the **second coming** of Jesus Christ. *See* also **Apostle / prophet in the market place; Fivefold ministry; Kingly believer; Who we are in Christ**

Kingdom of God: Kingdom is the Greek word *basileia* which means 'royal power, kingship, dominion', or the 'right or authority to rule over another kingdom'. This term therefore refers to the rule or government of God on the earth seen through the believers' kingship, power, dominion, right or **authority** given to them by the King of kings.

This kingdom can refer to two areas. (1) Any place God establishes His order and His way of doing things. In other words, anywhere His rule or dominion is physically seen in any of the **seven mountain kingdoms**. (2) The kingdom can also refer to a place in the **spiritual realm** where believers function from, since we are already seated with Christ in heavenly places according to Eph. 2: 6. **Kingdom now** refers to establishing this government now before Jesus physically brings it in its fullness on the earth. **Kingdom now and Kingdom of God movement** have been birthed from this principle (Dan. 4: 3; Matt. 3: 2; Luke 16: 16). See also **New Jerusalem.**

Kings and Priests Movement: See Kings and Priests.

Kings: This refers to believers who have been called by God into the office of a king in order produce money and wealth in order for the gospel to be preached. Kings function in the following anointing the **power to prosper,** fear and respect from people, favour, **special faith,** miracles to open financial doors, etc. (Deut. 8: 18, 28: 10). They will be responsible for closing huge business deals that would normally not be achieved, because they are empowered by God for His glory. Kings are driven by wisdom and the fear of the Lord (Prov. 8: 12–18, 21). Kings operate in the **gift of giving** and continual increase. These believers are called by God just like the **fivefold ministry**, and their function is a calling or ministry fully recognized by God just like any other ministry. Joseph, Daniel & Esther in the Bible are examples of this type of believer. (Ps. 1: 3; Rom. 12: 8, 13; Rev. 1: 6). See also **Seven Mountain Kingdoms.**

-L-

Last Hours/Days: See **End Times.**

Latter-Day Saints: See **Latter Rain.**

Latter Day: See **Latter Rain.**

Latter Rain Movement: See **Latter rain.**

Leading of the Holy Spirit: See **Yielding to the Holy Spirit.**

Leap of Faith: See **Acts/Actions of Faith.**

Latter Rain: This refers to a **Latter day** or **End-time** move or out-pouring of the Holy Spirit, referred to as the Latter rain. This outpouring will bring with it **revivals**, miracles, harvesting of souls and **prosperity** to the Church. This *Latter rain* is distinguished from the *former rain* as a fresh way in which God is going to pour out His Spirit on the earth. The **Latter rain movement** has come from this revelation. The teachings of the Latter rain movement put emphasis on believers walking in the **gifts of the Spirit, laying on of hands, restoration** of the **Fivefold ministry**, unity of the Church and so on. The Latter rain revelation also refers to the **Latter-Day Saints,** which are believers who will carry and manifest this Latter rain move (*This is not to be confused with the Church of Jesus Christ of Latter-day Saints*) (Joel 2: 23; Hos. 6: 3; Zech. 10: 1; James 5: 7).

Latter Wave: See **Third Day.**

Law of Sowing and Reaping: See **Sowing and Reaping.**

Laying on of Hands: This refers to the act of a believer physically putting hands on someone as a **point of contact** in order to release faith for something to happen to or for that person. Hands can be laid on someone for healing, an **operation of the Holy Spirit, prayer, impartation, activation,** etc. (Mark 16: 18; Acts 8: 17, 13: 3; 2 Tim. 1: 6).

Leadership: This is the ability to lead people or an organization in order to fulfil God's plans for the individuals and for that organization. It is one of the gifts of the Holy Spirit mentioned in Rom. 12:8. The **gift of leadership** empowers a believer with the ability to identify the gifts and talents of others and maximize those gifts for the Kingdom of God. Good leaders know how to put believers to fit in their place in order to fulfil their **membership role** in the **Body of Christ.** They know how to maximize the potential within a believer. Leaders are visionaries and strategists. The style and level of leadership will depend on the believers' **area of influence or calling.** Some are called to lead a few and others to lead thousands. *Administration* is often a fruit of this gift. Administrators are those with the ability to organize and plan. They have the ability to drive forward the objectives and goals of a ministry. The greatest key to good leadership is serving others according to Matthew 23: 11 and Mark 10: 44–45. Leadership in the style of **apostolic and prophetic leadership** is done through equipping, activating and releasing believers to fulfil their role in the Body of Christ. This is done by using the **apostolic and prophetic gifts.** See also **TEAR Programme.**

Leading of the Holy Spirit: See **Yielding to the Holy Spirit**

APOSTOLIC & PROPHETIC DICTIONARY

Leap of Faith: See **Acts/Actions of Faith**

Legal Right: See **Demonic/Forbidden Practices.**

Legalism: See **Religious Spirit.**

Lewdness: See **Debauchery/Lasciviousness.**

Life of God: See *Zoe.*

Local Church: See **Church.**

Logos: It is a Greek translation from *word.* The *logos* is used to refer to the canonized scriptures as they are contained in the sixty-six books of the Bible as the ultimate and highest authority of truth on earth. The *logos* is the written **Word of God** (John 17: 17; 2 Tim. 3: 16–17; 2 Pet. 1: 20–21). See also **Doctrine;** *Rhema;* **Teaching.**

Longsuffering: See **Patience/Longsuffering.**

Love: This is the main nature and characteristic of God and should be for every believer. Love is the main **fruit of the Spirit** because the other eight find their place in love. Love is also a commandment given to all believers to walk in. Love for God (not His blessings) and His people is one of the great keys for believers to walk in the power of God in these last days (John 3: 16; 15: 9–17; 1 Cor. 13: 4–8; Gal. 5: 13; 22–23; 1 John 4: 7–12). See also **Character.**

-M-

Magic/Witchcraft/Sorcery: See **Demonic/Forbidden Practices.**

Mandate: See **Calling.**

Manifest Sons of God Movement: See **Manifest Sons of God.**

Manifest Sons of God: This refers to a people that God is raising to operate like Jesus did on the earth. This revelation focuses on believers seeing themselves as sons and daughters of God endued with the same Holy Spirit and the same rights as the Son of God, Jesus Christ. The **manifest sons of God movement** has come from this revelation. This movement is similar to the **Latter rain movement** (John 1: 12; Rom. 8: 19; Gal. 3: 26; 1 John 3: 1). See also **Sons of God**

Manifestation: This means to 'reveal' or 'bring out into the natural something that is in the supernatural or spiritual realm'. It can relate to the promises of God, demons, or angels. Manifestation put differently is the 'seen physical evidence of the things that are unseen'. See also **Faith; Spiritual Realm; Supernatural.**

Mantle: It is derived from the meaning of 'to cover', as in a blanket or coat. It is an anointing that covers a believer. A mantle is unique or specific to the believer it rests upon. It cannot be shared or given while the believer is still alive or on the earth because it is what

God has clothed the believer with to operate with while on the earth. It is his or her personal and unique anointing, gifts, or *grace* (2 Kings 2: 9–13, 13: 21). This word mantle can be used in some of the following ways:

(1) **Placing a demand on the mantle/anointing,** which means to recognise the anointing that accompanies the mantle of another believer and by faith placing an expectation for the anointing that flows with that mantle to be released. Many people did this in the Bible and received healings, and other blessings (2 Kings 2: 9; Mark 5: 25–34).

(2) **Honouring the mantle/anointing,** which means to intentionally recognise and respect the mantle with its anointing upon another believer. This honour is expressed through words and actions that intentionally pay tribute to the man or woman of God. This can result in God releasing a blessing that is upon that mantle (2 Kings 4: 8–17; Matt. 10: 41–42).

(3) **Taking up the mantle,** which means carrying on with the mantle of a man or woman of God, from where they have stopped on the earth. This may involve carrying on with their doctrine, gifts and callings (2 Kings 2: 9–15). See also **Honouring Man and Woman of God.**

Many Are Called but Few Are Chosen: See **Preparation of a Man and Woman of God.**

Marketplace: This is any area outside the **local church** which involves trading, industry or business. Market place ministers are therefore those believers who take the gospel to work places, public places, and areas of trade and industry. *See* also **Apostle/Prophet in the Marketplace; Kings; Seven Mountain Kingdoms.**

Marriage Supper of the Lamb: This refers to a feast and a time of celebration for Christ and His Church, that will occur after His **Second Coming**. Only **believers** qualify for this ceremony (Rev. 19: 7–9).

Meditation: This is the process by which a believer focuses on a certain scripture, teaching or concept from God in order to get **revelation** from it and allow it to become part of their thinking and **faith**. To meditate put differently is to chew and digest on the Word in order to obtain a richer and fuller meaning from it. Instead of reading the Bible in chapters, meditation often focuses on certain verses. It is a necessary way to change the Bible from being mere information to becoming **revelation** that results in **faith** and **spiritual growth**. Meditation also results in the **renewing of the mind** of a believer. This means to change the old ways of thinking based on the flesh and the devil, in order to begin thinking according to the thought patterns of God (Josh. 1: 8; Prov. 23: 7; Rom. 12: 2; Phil. 4: 8). See also **Repentance**.

Meekness: See **Gentleness/Meekness**.

Membership Role/Ministry: See **Body of Christ**.

Message: This refers to a specific **doctrine**, teaching or **revelation** that God has given to a believer to teach and preach to the Body of Christ as their unique mandate or assignment. A believer may teach on various aspects of the Bible but their Message is usually what forms the main focus or the majority of their teachings. For example, a believers' message can focus on one or more of these Biblical concepts: **Prosperity, healing, deliverance, Fivefold ministry,** marriage, etc. The message is given by God as part of a believer's spirit and it is what drives their calling (Jer. 1: 5, 10; Acts 9: 15). See also **Assignment; Mandate**.

Mid-Tribulation Rapture: See **Rapture.**

Millennial Era: This refers to the one thousand years in which Christ will establish His rule on earth after the defeat of the **false prophet** and the beast. It is also called the **millennial rule** or **millennial kingdom**. In this time the devil will be locked away and released after a thousand years to deceive people for the last time. After this time, Jesus Christ will cast him into the lake of fire forever and bring the **New Jerusalem** on the earth (Rev. 20: 1–10).

There are three different ways in which this concept is viewed.

(1) **Post-Millennialism:** This view suggests that Christ will only return after the Church has rooted out evil through preaching and teaching.

(2) **A-Millennialism:** This view suggests that the Millennium is already in the process and that the thousand years referred to in the Bible is merely symbolic and not literal.

(3) **Pre-Millennialism:** This view suggests that the thousand years is a literal number of years that Christ will establish His kingdom on earth. This seems to be the most accepted view, and it is the view that forms the main explanation. See also **Eschatology.**

Ministry: This word comes from the verb 'minister', which has the meaning of 'to serve, attend, aid support, or care for'. A ministry is therefore, any institution or act of service, aid or support towards the work of God and the gospel of Jesus Christ. All believers are ministers in one way or another, because all believers have been called to serve Jesus Christ. Rom. 12: 7 however mentions ministry as a gift. The **gift of ministry** is specifically given to certain believers whom God has given greater grace to serve Him as well as others. See also **Body of Christ; Fruit of the Spirit.**

Miracle: This is the supernatural intervention of God in a natural situation. When a miracle happens it cannot be explained by human reason. This is because it is Divine and comes from the God who has no limitations and is not governed by any natural laws. Constant manifestation of miracles should be a part of every believer's life. There are a wide range of miracles involving every area of life, from multiplication of products, to **translations**, to controlling the weather and elements, debt cancellations, supernatural provision etc. There are no limits in the realm of miracles, because there are no limits to what God can do for and through a believer that is within His Word. The **gift of miracles** is a gift given to some believers to manifest miracles (Ex. 16: 14–35; Josh. 6: 6–20; 1 Kin. 17: 14–24; Matt. 14: 34–36; John 2: 1–11; John 21: 6). See also **Creative Miracles; Signs and Wonders; Supernatural.**

Miracle Money/Wealth: This refers to the supernatural appearing of money or valuables for believers. It can mean money appearing in bank accounts, multiplying in wallets, debt cancellations, etc. This is one of the major signs of the transfer of wealth taking place. See also **End-Time Transfer of Wealth; Prosperity.**

Movement: This is a specific way in which the Holy Spirit moves in a certain place, time or season, with a specific set of people on the earth. We can better understand a Holy Spirit inspired movement by looking at its characteristics, which may include the following:

(1) It is always initiated or started by God. God starts movements when He wants to establish certain aspects of His will or Word on the earth.

(2) God uses pioneers and fathers on the earth to begin and nature the movement. It may be one or several.

APOSTOLIC & PROPHETIC DICTIONARY

(3) It is based on scripture and **sound doctrine**.

(4) It may take time to be accepted but it eventually becomes part of the revelation caught by the general **Body of Christ**. A movement usually has with it a large number who accept the revelation and move with it.

(5) It comes with the demonstration of what it teaches. It's validity must be confirmed with manifestations.

(6) It is usually followed by books, teachings, and resources to clarify what the movement is about.

Examples of past and present movements and the truth restored include The **Protestant movement** which brought restoration of salvation by grace and not through works, opposed or protested the then long standing Roman Catholic doctrines. (Hence the name 'Protestant'). They were also called Lutherans (named after pioneer Martin Luther). The **Evangelical movement** brought about the emphasis of water baptism by immersion. The **Holiness movement** brought the restoration of believers living a sanctified life (also called 'Methodist' due to the methods they employed in living according to the principles that they believed in). The **faith-healing movement** brought the restoration of healing as a promise for every believer. The **Pentecostal movement,** brought the restoration of the experience that occurred on the day of Pentecost in Acts 2, which brought the indwelling presence of the Holy Spirit with evidence of speaking in new tongues. (Hence the name 'Pentecostals'.) The **charismatic movement** brought the restoration of the other **gifts of the Spirit**. (The Greek word for gifts is 'charisma', hence the term 'Charismatic'.) The **faith movement** brought about the restoration on faith in the Word, and the promises of prosperity and healing, for every believer. The **prophetic movement,** brought with it the restoration of the office of the **prophet** and the **prophetic gifts**. The **apostolic movement,** brought the restoration of the office of the **apostle** and the **apostolic gifts.** The name of the movement should not matter, as long as it is supported by the scriptures. Some movements may have the same essential message but have different names depending on the revelation which is given by God to the founders or pioneers. For example, the **kings and priests movement, dominion movement,** and the **manifest sons of God movement** all emphasize believers taking over the earth for Jesus and manifesting His **power** and **authority.** Believers should not get caught up in names of movements but in the message behind them. See also **Present Truth; Restoration.**

-N-

Nabi: See **Prophet**.

Names of God: The name of **God** or His personal name is JHVH or YHWH (it is the name LORD written in capital letters in the Bible). This is hard to pronounce. so we have come to call Him Jehovah or Yahweh. This means 'I am that I am'. This is the name He gave Moses in Exodus 3: 14 as His name. The name I am that I am means the 'Self-Existent One', or 'the One who continually reveals Himself'. In other words, *there can be no single name that can describe God*. We know Him as He reveals Himself. This is the reason He has so many names in the Bible, because each one of them reveals Him in a different way.

These Following are some of His Hebrew names according to the Bible.

(1) *Elohim,* which means God (Gen. 1: 1).
(2) *Adonai,* which means Lord or Master (Mal. 1: 6).
(3) *Jehovah/Yahweh,* which means Self-Existent One (Gen. 2: 4).
(4) *Jehovah–Maccaddeshem,* which means the Lord your sanctifier (Ex. 31: 13).
(5) *Jehovah–Rohi,* which means the Lord your shepherd (Ps. 23: 1).
(6) *Jehovah–Shamah,* which means the Lord who is present (Ezek. 48: 35).

(7) *Jehovah-Rapha*, which means the Lord your healer (Ex. 15: 26).

(8) *Jehovah-Tsidkenu*, which means the Lord your righteousness (Jer. 23: 6).

(9) *Jehovah-Jireh*, which means the Lord your provider (Gen. 22: 13–14).

(10) *Jehohav-Nissi*, which means the Lord your banner (Ex. 17: 15).

(11) *Jehovah-Shalom* which means The Lord your peace. (Judg. 6: 24).

(12) *Jehovah-Sabbaoth*, which means the Lord of Hosts of the armies of heaven (Isa. 6: 1–3).

(13) *El-Elyon*, which means the Most High God (Isa. 14: 13–14).

(14) *El-Roi*, which means the Strong One who sees (Gen. 16: 13).

(15) *El-Shaddai*, which means God who is all sufficient (Gen. 17: 1; Ps. 91: 1).

(16) *El-Olam*, which means Everlasting God (Gen. 21: 33).

(17) *Yeshhau*, which means the Lord is **salvation**. This is the name of Jesus. His name encompasses or includes all these saving attributes of God. In Jesus all of these virtues of God are found.

Believers should study these names and trust God to reveal all of them in their lives. It is important to know these names for the following reasons: Through them God meets every need we have and the world has. A believer can use a certain name to bring that side of Him to manifest. Through them we learn how to worship and honour Him. Only His names can reveal who He is, and worshiping Him for who He is pleases Him. *See* also **Godhead/Trinity; Omni Attributes of God.**

Networks: This refers to any interactions and connections in the **kingdom of God** intended for the sharing of resources and information in order to have a larger impact. *See* also **Apostolic and Prophetic Networks; Partnership/Partnering**

New Age: This refers to the popular belief system arising in the world today based on Eastern religions and rituals. It's followers are called New Agers. All New Age practices emanate from **witchcraft,** the **occult** and satan and are therefore strictly forbidden for believers. The **New Age movement** has come from this concept (Deut. 18: 9–12; Isa. 2: 6). See **also Demonic/Forbidden Practices.**

New Covenant: See **Covenant.**

New Creation: See **Born Again.**

New Jerusalem: This refers to the heavenly city that God will bring from heaven to earth after the **millennial era.** God will live with us in this new city, and there will be no need for the sun or moon because He will be the light (Rev. 21: 1–5). See also **Eschatology.**

New Man: See **Born Again.**

New Wine Movement: See **New Wine.**

New Wine: This refers to a movement of the Holy Spirit that Jesus is releasing for His church in these last days. This revelation is based on the parable given by Jesus in Matt. 9: 14–17 and Luke 5: 33–39. The old wine skins compared to the New Wine skins represents a *new type* of believers who are living a life devoted to God and ready to receive what is new and cutting–edge from the Holy Spirit. This revelation of the New Wine has been evidenced by operations of the Holy Spirit like **holy laughter,** where believers laugh uncontrollably as inspired by the Holy Spirit. It is also evidenced by believers being **drunk in the Spirit,** which is where believers lose control of their faculties and behaviour as moved by the Holy Spirit. The **new wine movement** is based on this revelation. See also **Fresh Anointing; Revival.**

New Truths: See **Present Truths.**

-O-

Occult: It is derived from the Latin word *occultus,* which means 'things hidden, things in darkness, the practices of divination, and sorcery'. All forms of occult practices form part of **demonic/forbidden practices.** *See* also **Antichrist; Deliverance; Satan/Demons.**

Offering: Offering is anything of value given to God. It can be praise and worship but it can also be material or financial offerings. Offering is a powerful way of releasing devotion and **faith** in order for God to move on your behalf. Being generous should be part of a believer's life (Luke 6: 38; Acts: 10: 1–4; 2 Cor. 9: 7; Heb. 13: 16). See also **Giving; Kings; Prosperity; Sacrificial Giving; Tithes.**

Old Covenant: See **Covenant.**

Omega Generation: This refers to the generation or people that will be involved in the final move of God on the earth. The word *omega* comes from the Greek word, which is used to denote the last, the end or the limit of something. This is a generation of believers who believe that, they will usher in the **Second Coming** of Jesus Christ by fulfilling the final call and mandate of God on the earth. It is also called the **finishing generation** (Rev. 1: 8; 21: 6).

Omni Attributes of God: Generally God bears three characteristics that are unique to Him. They are called the *omni* attributes. *Omni* in

Latin means all. No other human, angel, god, or demon including satan has these qualities.

(1) *Omnipotent*, which means He is all powerful. God is limitless in power. He can do whatever He wants when He wants (Job 42: 2; Matt. 19: 26).

(2) *Omniscient*, which means He is all knowing. There is nothing in heaven or on earth that is hidden from God. He has infinite or limitless knowledge (Job 37: 16; Hebrews 4: 13; 1 John 3: 20).

(3) *Omnipresent*, which means He is all present or present everywhere at the same time. He fills heaven and earth at the same time (Ps. 139: 7–12; Jer. 23: 24). See also **Godhead/ Trinity; Names of God.**

Omnipotent: See **Omni Attributes of God**

Omnipresent: See **Omni Attributes of God**

Omniscient: See **Omni Attributes of God**

Once Saved Always Saved: This is the view that once a person becomes **born again** and receives his or her **salvation,** he or she can never go to hell no matter how much the person sin or rebel against God. It is based on the view that believers did nothing to earn their salvation and can therefore do nothing to lose it (John 10: 28; Rom. 8: 37–39; 1 John 5: 13). See also **Carnal Christian/Believer; Holiness; Unforgiveness.**

Open Doors: This refers to opportunities or ways that have been opened by God. These open doors usually come in the way of favour in the eyes of people (Rev. 3: 8). See also **God's Timing.**

Open-Eye Vision/Open Vision: See **Vision.**

Open Heaven: See **Glory.**

Operation of the Holy Spirit: This refers to a certain way in which the Holy Spirit functions or moves in the natural. Different operations are for example people being **slain**, falling one by one or many at a time, vibrating, feeling heat, a wind, electricity or tingling feeling etc. These form part of God's **signs and wonders.**

Ordination: This refers to the process of being ordained, which ordinarily means to be *appointed, set apart, put in place* or *instituted* for something. However a much more significant meaning is to be *bestowed the power or authority to minister.* Ordination in this sense is usually done by elders who lay hands and officially recognize the person to a place of leadership and ministry. Ordination by the elders is a recognition of what God has already given from before birth. Although not mandatory, ordination is necessary because it is an order and a structure put by the Holy Spirit in order to send out His leaders. Ordination is usually done in front of a church congregation and other elders in an *ordination service* (Jer. 1: 5; Acts 14: 23; Titus 1: 5). See also **Commission; Covering; God's release.**

Original Sin: See **Fall of Man.**

Orphan Spirit/Mindset: See **Sons of God.**

-P-

Parakletos: See **Exhort/Exhortation.**

Partner: See **Partnership/Partnering.**

Partnership/Partnering: This refers to any way in which a **partner** which is a believer or ministry supports or connects with another ministry. This can be done in three main ways:

(1) Supporting the ministry financially or with other material resources.
(2) Praying and interceding for that ministry.
(3) Attending the ministries' events and functions especially to participate as a volunteer.

Partnership in the aspect of supporting a ministry financially either once off or regularly in order to receive the anointing upon that ministry is often referred to as **sowing into an anointing.** Partnership has several advantages such as, financial blessings, **spiritual covering,** ministry promotion and for receiving the anointing that is upon that ministry (Eccl. 4: 9; 1 Cor. 3: 9; Gal. 6: 6–9). See also **Networks.**

Pastor: This is one of the **Fivefold** offices mentioned in Ephesians 4: 11. The word pastor is Latin derived from the word *poimen* in the Greek, and it directly means a *shepherd.* It is *roeh* in the Hebrew and has the meaning of 'feeding a flock'. Pastors have been given the unique ability to care for, protect and feed those whose lives they are responsible for. Pastors also act as overseers who manage the **local church** by governing its day to day affairs. The gifts, grace or anointing that follow the pastor are usually **compassion** and **teaching**. More and more pastors are however increasingly moving in the **apostolic and prophetic gifts**. A **Senior pastor** refers to the most senior in position at the local church. It also usually refers to the founder of a local church (Jer. 3: 15; John 21: 16; 1 Pet. 5: 1–2). See also **Fivefold Ministry.**

Patience/Longsuffering: This is one of the **fruit of the Spirit.** It is the Greek word *makrothumia,* which means 'forbearance or patient endurance'. It describes a person who has the ability to endure ill-treatment and persecution. Or a person who can exercise revenge but chooses not to. Another Greek word is *hupomone,* which means *to remain under difficulties and still have the hope that resists weariness and giving up* (Eph. 4: 2; Col. 1: 11; 2 Tim. 2: 24; Heb. 10: 36). See also **Character; Perseverance/Endurance.**

Paying the Price for the Calling: This refers to the preparation process, hardships, persecution, etc. which a believer voluntarily yields to if necessary in order to complete the calling, assignment or mandate given to them by God (Luke 14: 26–33). See also **Calling; Preparation of a Man or Woman of God.**

Peace: This is one of the **fruit of the Spirit**. It comes from the Greek word *eirene* and the Hebrew word *shalom*. Both words have the meaning of a state of reaching rest, as a result of a relationship with God. It also means 'wholeness, completeness, or tranquillity within the believer that is unaffected by the outward circumstances or pressures'. With this fruit of the Spirit believers are able to stay calm and in faith in the midst of unsettling, traumatic and chaotic situations. Prince of peace is one of the names of Jesus Christ. This means one of His roles is to produce this peace within the believer (Isa. 9: 6; 26: 3; John 16: 33; 2 Thess. 3: 16). See also **Character; Fear.**

Pentecostal Movement: See **Movement.**

Persecution: See **Trials /Tests/Tribulations /Sufferings.**

Perseverance/Endurance: This is the ability to continue in a God given direction which is given either through the *logos* or *rhema*, despite difficulties and opposition. It is also called pressing-on, or to press-on towards the goal. (Phil. 3: 14). Believers must persevere in order to walk into the fulfilment of God's promises for their lives (Gal. 6: 9; Heb. 6: 10–11). See also **God's Timing; Fruit of the Spirit: Trials/Tests/ Tribulations /Sufferings.**

Personal Anointing: See **Anointing.**

Personal Prophecy: This is a prophetic message that applies to a person concerning their lives and the plan God has for them. They are personal or unique for the person who receives them. They can be given concerning any area of a person's life for example marriage, children, calling etc. Believers must welcome accurate personal prophecies, write them down and trust God to fulfil them in their lives. Personal prophecies can be given through **prophets, prophetic ministers** and through other ways in which God speaks, for example **dreams, visions,** angelic **visitations** etc. Believers who encourage and embrace personal prophecies find it easier to reach their God given destiny. Believers must therefore encourage and welcome personal prophecies and must seek to give others prophetic messages (Acts

21: 10–11; 2 Chron. 20: 20; 2 Kings 4: 16; 1 Tim. 1: 18, 4: 14). See also **Journaling; Prophetic Gifts; Prophetic Presbytery;** *Rhema.*

Placing a Demand on the Mantle/Anointing: See **Mantle.**

Pleading the Blood: This refers to the faith statement made over a situation to invoke the power found in the blood of Jesus Christ. The blood of Jesus Christ has not only removed all sin, but has made believers enter into a covenant filled with blessings and promises from God. Pleading the blood of Jesus Christ or covering a situation under the blood is a powerful way of calling upon the rights and privileges that we have in the New Testament. These include protection, **prosperity, healing**, wholeness, etc. (Ex. 12: 13; 1 John1: 7; Rev. 12: 11). See also **Salvation.**

Point of Contact: This refers to any physical object or place where faith in God can be released to obtain an answer. A point of contact can include some of the following: Taking something for example a *piece of cloth, anointing-oil, glass of water* or going somewhere for example *attending a service,* It can also include releasing or letting go of something for example *money, a book, an object,* etc. (Mark 5: 28; Acts 19: 11–12). See also **Faith; Laying on of Hands.**

Post-Millennialism: See **Millennial Era.**

Post-Tribulation Rapture: See **Rapture.**

Power Evangelism/Witnessing: This refers to evangelizing or witnessing to people about Jesus by using the power of the Holy Spirit through the **apostolic gifts** and the **prophetic gifts** (this is more commonly called **prophetic evangelism**) and **signs and wonders**. This concept is derived from the fact that God confirms His word with accompanying signs (Mark 16: 17–20; 1 Cor. 2: 4). See also **Demonstrations of the Holy Spirit.**

Power gifts: See **Gifts of the Spirit.**

Power to Prosper: This refers to the gift, grace or anointing given to a believer to produce prosperity. **Prosperity** means to have *success* and *well-fare* in every area of life. Prosperity is the will of God for all believers who desire it (2 Cor. 8: 9; Phil. 4: 19; 3 John 2). Although all believers can access abundance and wealth through faith, some believers are uniquely chosen by God to produce wealth to finance the **kingdom of God** (Deut. 8: 18). See also **Kings.**

Practising the Presence of God: This refers to activities or exercises which are done by the believer in order to better hear and listen to the voice of God. Some of these activities include time in **prayer, meditation, praise and worship, journaling,** etc. Every believer should be able to hear and speak the heart and mind or God (John 10: 27). See also **Interpretation of tongues; Prophetic gifts; Seeking the face/heart of God**

Power of God: This word *power* comes from the Greek word '*dunamis*' which means the *miraculous ability, power,* or *force of God. Dunamis* is where the word *dynamic* is derived from. Dynamic means *energy, functioning, alive, operating* or *working.* The power of God is alive, functioning and always operating, which means it will always produce productivity and change in the life of a believer and in the lives of others. The English word *dynamite* also comes from the word *dunamis. Dunamis* is the explosive power of God which breaks natural and demonic limitations and circumstances (for example sickness, sin, weakness, curses, poverty, lack of progress etc.). The source of *dunamis* is the Word of God and the producer of *dunamis* is the Holy Spirit. (Acts 1: 8; Heb. 4: 12) See also **Demonstrations of the Holy Spirit**

Praise and worship: These are two distinct acts of honour to God, and the best way to understand them is to look at their characteristics and differences.

(1) Praise is *loud and vibrant*. Worship is *deep and intimate*.

(2) Praise speaks more of *what God has done*. Worship speaks more of *who God is*.

(3) Praise *sets up the throne* of God and worship *bows before that throne*.

(4) Praise gives God *thanksgiving, rejoicing* and *gratitude*. Worship gives God *reverence, love devotion* and *humility*. (5) Praise is accompanied by physical acts such as *clapping, dancing, shouting, jumping, screaming, playing different sounds and instruments* etc. Worship is accompanied by physical acts such as *kneeling, silence, weeping, repentance, meditation, raising of hands, acts of service, obedience, recommitment to God*, etc.

(6) Praise is more a *fruit from the lips*. Worship is more a *fruit from the heart*. Praise and worship should form part of a believer's daily walk with God: **Praise** (Ps. 22: 3; 33: 2–3; 95: 1–2; 100: 4; 103: 1–4; 150: 1–6) and **Worship** (1 Chr. 16: 11; Ps. 95: 6; John 4: 23–24). See also **Seeking the Face/Heart of God.**

Prayer: This refers to any communication between a believer or believers and God. Prayers are sent to the Father in the name of Jesus Christ. (John 14: 6; 13–14; Eph. 3: 14–21; Heb. 4: 14–16). There are different kinds of prayer, which include

(1) **Meditation**

(2) **Intercession**

(3) **Praise and worship**

(4) **Faith confessions/decrees/declarations**

(5) Praying through the **gift of tongues**

(6) **Prayer of consecration**, which can also be called the prayer of surrender, which is prayed where a believer rededicates his or her life to God. With this prayer we choose to die to self and live in Christ (Matt. 26: 36–42; Phil. 3: 7–10; Gal. 2: 20).

(7) **Prayer of agreement**, is the prayer where two or more believers join their faith in order to receive a certain answer from God (Matt. 18: 18–20).

(8) **Prayer of supplication/asking** which is when believers' bring their needs before God in order to be answered. God encourages believers to ask Him because He desires to answer. Sometimes this prayer can be prayed as a deep cry to God in a desperate situation (1 Sam. 1: 1–20: Mark 11: 24; Luke 11: 9–10).

(9) **Prayer of confession/repentance**, is used when a believer has sinned against God. All sins must be confessed to God in order to receive His forgiveness (1 John 1: 9).

(10) **Prayer to command** is the prayer where the believer uses their **authority** in Jesus in order to command or decree the result they want to see in the natural realm. This prayer is used in cases such as casting out demons and rebuking a sicknesses or disease (Mark 11: 23; Luke 10: 19).

Prayer of Agreement: See **Prayer.**

Prayer of Confession/Repentance: See **Prayer.**

Prayer of Supplication/Asking: See **Prayer.**

Prayer to Command: See **Prayer.**

Prayer Walks: See **Intercession.**

Prayer Watch: See **Intercession.**

Praying for the Lost: See **Intercession.**

Pre-Millennialism: See **Millennial Era.**

Preparation of a Man or Woman of God: This refers to the process undertaken by God in order to perfect the **character** and **spiritual maturity** of a believer who wishes to move in their **callings** and **gifts.** This process usually involves numerous character building experiences through a God ordained time period or **time of preparation. God** determines when they will start and when they will stop. God also permits these times in our lives in order to develop the **fruit of the Spirit** and Godly **character** within the believer. Every believer who desires to serve God in ministry and in their calling must allow God to start and finish this process. It is a Biblical principle that those called to make the most impact for God undergo the most preparation (Luke 12: 48*).* In Matt. 22: 14, Jesus says **many are called but few are chosen**. This means God has a calling for every believer and desires for them to walk in it. However few actually get chosen or approved by God to walk in the fullness of that calling. This is as a result of not allowing God to shape the necessary character and maturity needed to execute their calling. This preparation may happen in different periods of a believer's life (Heb. 12: 2–11; 1 Pet. 1: 6–7; 5: 10). See also **God's Timing; Perseverance/Endurance.**

Prepare the Way: This refers to the preparations that the Church of Jesus Christ have to make with the Holy Spirit in order to usher in the

Second Coming. These include but are not limited to **winning souls** for **end-time harvest,** various **restoration movements** of **present truths,** collecting the **end-time transfer of wealth,** etc. Jesus Christ is **coming soon** means the period left for the Second Coming is near. This is evidenced by the prophetic scriptures fulfilled by world events taking place (Isa. 40: 3; Mal. 3: 1; Phil. 4: 5; Rev. 3: 11; 22: 7). See also **Elijah Spirit; Eschatology; Rapture.**

Present Truths: This refers to relevant scriptural truths for the Church, for the present season or time, as they are revealed by the Holy Spirit. Often these truths are revealed and made known to the Church through **apostolic and prophetic pioneers.** The phrase **new truths** is similar, but refers more to fresh **revelation** based on the Word of God that is given and taught as led by the Holy Spirit. See also **Restoration; Revelation; *Rhema*.**

Pre-Tribulation Rapture: See **Rapture.**

Pre-Wrath Rapture: See **Rapture.**

Priestly Believer: This refers to a believer who has the anointing, gifts or grace of one of the **Fivefold ministry,** but does not necessarily function in one of those offices. This type of believer preaches or ministers part-time and focuses on a business or job as their main area of influence and calling. See also **Kingly Believer; Kings and Priests.**

Prophecy: It comes from the Greek word *propheteuo*, which means 'to foretell'. It can also mean to *declare something which is divinely revealed*. Prophecy refers to anytime the Holy Spirit communicates the heart and mind of God for a particular person, place or situation. Prophecy can apply to the past, present or the future. When a prophecy is given it can carry within it some or all of the other three **prophetic gifts.** The **gift of prophecy** is a gift of the Holy Spirit which enables a believer to prophesy. To **prophesy** is to speak forth that which is divinely revealed by God. (Joel 2: 28; Luke 1: 67–80; John 4: 16–19; Acts 2: 16–20; 21: 9). See also **Prophet.**

Prophesy: See **Prophecy.**

Prophet in the Marketplace: See **Apostle/Prophet in the Marketplace.**

Prophet: This is one of the Fivefold ministries and also a foundational office. Prophets are watchmen and the Lord entrusts them with the responsibility of hearing and declaring His heart and mind for people, nations, situations, and seasons. The prophet's office is usually accompanied by the anointing, gift or grace of **prophecy, word of knowledge, word of wisdom** and **discerning of spirits** (1 Cor. 12: 8–10). Prophets have the grace to open up new levels within believers and over regions and nations. This is because prophets speak the very Word of God which moves with the Spirit's power and angelic hosts to manifest it.

There are generally four types of prophets, or four main ways prophets receive prophetic messages from God.

(1) **Hearer**: This type hears from God either through a still small voice or an audible voice. They can also hear from angels.

(2) **Seer**: This type mainly sees pictures or images, through trances dreams and visions.

(3) **Feeler/knower**: This type feels or knows that God wants to say or do something.

(4) *Nabi*: This type of prophet speaks and God fills their mouth. The prophecies bubble forth or flow as they speak; they usually have no form of revelation until they speak.

False prophets are prophets who are driven by **false doctrine** and often pursue self-centred ambitions (Matt. 24: 24). False prophets can be influenced by their flesh but also by satanic powers (1 Cor. 12: 28; Eph. 2: 20; 4: 11; 1 John 4: 1–6). See also **Fivefold Ministry.**

Prophetic: See **Apostolic and Prophetic**

Prophetic Acts/Actions: This refers to when a believer performs certain actions in the physical to represent what they want to see happen in the **spiritual realm**. For example using hands to pull down property from heaven, or rolling on the floor to represent rolling over the nations for God. This may be led by the Holy Spirit or performed by the believer in faith. See also **Acts/Actions of Faith.**

Prophetic Art: This refers to the inspiration given by the Holy Spirit to a believer in order to produce a piece of artist work in the physical realm. It can be a painting, drawing, sculpture, etc.

Prophetic Believer/Minister: This refers to a believer who moves or functions in the anointing, gifts or grace that accompany the prophet without being a prophet. All believers must be prophetic, meaning all must be able to hear God and speak forth His revealed word. See also **Journaling; Practising the Presence of God; Prophet; Prophetic Gifts.**

Prophetic Counselling: This refers to counselling conducted through the use of the **prophetic gifts**. This type of counselling is the most effective because the believer counselling identifies and solves any problems a person may have supernaturally by the power of God. See also **Discerning of Spirits; Prophet; Prophetic Gifts; Word of Knowledge; Word of Wisdom.**

Prophetic Dance: This refers to a dance or bodily movement which is inspired by the Holy Spirit (2 Sam. 6: 14).

Prophetic Evangelism: See **Power Evangelism/Witnessing**

Prophetic Gifts: This refers to the gifts of the Holy Spirit that accompany the office of prophet of prophetic believers. They include **word of knowledge, word of wisdom, prophecy** and **discerning of spirits**. Prophetic gifts are available for all believers by faith (1 Cor. 12: 8–10). See also **Prophet.**

Prophetic Insight: See **Apostolic and Prophetic Order.**

Prophetic Intercession: See **Intercession.**

Prophetic Ministry: See **Apostolic and Prophetic Ministries.**

Prophetic Praise and Worship: This refers to when a believer is inspired to praise and worship God in a specific way as led by the Holy Spirit. This is usually done in order for God to accomplish something specific (2 Chron. 20: 15–25; Josh. 6: 16–21). See also **Prophetic Prayer.**

Prophetic Prayer: This is when the believer is inspired to pray for certain things that God has revealed to them either for their own lives or for others. The latter is called **prophetic intercession.** Many times prophetic prayer and prophetic praise and worship will result in **prophetic spiritual warfare.** This is where God uses the prayers and the praise of the believer to bring down **demonic strongholds**

in their own lives or elsewhere. It can be over other people, places countries and continents. All believers who have a call for intercession should press into these gifts and function in them for effective and accurate prayer. As much as all believers are called to intercede. There are others who have this burden from God more than others.

Prophetic presbytery: This is when two or more **prophets** and /or **prophetic ministers** lay hands on and prophesy over individuals at a specified time and place.

Prophetic presbyteries are conducted for several reasons:

(1) For revealing the calling on the believer.
(2) For a *rhema* word in order to bring direction.
(3) For **impartation** and **activation** of anointing, gifts, graces, and callings.
(4) To bring revelation, clarification, and confirmation of leadership ministry in the local church.
(5) For the **laying on of hands** and **prophecy** over those called and properly prepared to be in the **Fivefold ministry** (Acts 13: 1–4; 1 Tim. 4: 14). See also **Commissioning; Ordination.**

Prophetic Song: This refers to when the Holy Spirit inspires a believer with the words to a song, either to sing or to write down. The song may be sung in public or in a private time with God. This type of gift may also be in the form of *prophetic psalms*, or *poems* to God.

Prophetic Spiritual Warfare: See **Prophetic Prayer**

Prophetic Teams: See **Apostolic and Prophetic Teams.**

Prophet's Reward: This refers to a blessing or reward that believers receive by honouring the mantle or anointing that is on a **prophet**

of God or his or her prophecies, usually by acting on their word and by accepting it as a word from God (2 Chron. 20: 20; Matt. 10: 41). See also **Honouring Leaders; Personal Prophecy.**

Prosperity: See **Power to Prosper.**

Protestant Movement: See **Movement.**

Pursuing Holiness: See **Holiness.**

-R-

Rapture: This refers to an event of the snatching away of the Church and believers from earth in order to meet Jesus in mid-air. The word rapture, which is not actually found in the English Bible, is an English word which comes from the Latin *rapiemur,* or *rapere,* which means to 'snatch away'. It has been translated from the Greek word *harpagisometha* or *harpaz,* which means to be 'caught up'. The rapture is not the **Second Coming** of Christ because during the rapture, Jesus does not physically come to earth but remains in midair, where we will be 'caught up' to meet Him. The Second Coming is the time when Jesus comes to earth to judge the **antichrist,** the **false prophet,** and satan and his demons, and to establish His kingdom physically on earth. There are some who believe that the rapture will occur before the **Great Tribulation.** This theory is called **pre-tribulation rapture.** Some believe in the middle of the tribulation, or in a **mid-tribulation rapture.** Some believe it will be before the wrath of Christ on the earth or in a **pre-wrath rapture.** Then there are others who believe it will be after the Great-tribulation, or a **post-tribulation rapture.** There seems to be scriptures to support all of these theories and a believer should make up their own mind. Regardless of the time of the rapture all believers have a responsibility to live a life that is holy and pleasing before God in order to be a part of it (Matt. 24: 42; 1 Cor. 15: 51–52; 1 Thess. 4: 16–18, 5: 2,23). See also **Eschatology.**

Realm of the Spirit: See **Spiritual Realm.**

Receptive to the Holy Spirit: This refers to the level of sensitivity a believer has to the communication of God given by the Holy Spirit to them. God is always talking to believers and He desires for all to hear His voice and to obey it (John 10: 27, 14: 26, 16: 12–14). See also **Conviction of the Holy Spirit; Yielding to the Holy Spirit.**

Redeemed: This refers to the state of being bought back from spiritual death and the fallen world by the blood sacrifice of Jesus Christ on the cross. Jesus paid a terrible price for our sins, and through His blood we know belong to Him and all the rights of His promises belong to believers, the devil and all that came with the curse and **fall of man,** such as spiritual death, lack, poverty, illness etc. no longer have a right to operate in the life of a believer (Rom. 3:24; Eph. 1:7; Col. 1:14). See **Born-Again; Salvation**

Redeemed from the Curse of the Law: See **Abraham's Blessing.**

Regional Spirits: See **Strongholds.**

Releasing the Supernatural: See **Supernatural.**

Releasing: See **TEAR Programme.**

Religious Spirit: This refers to the mind-set that relies on laws and traditions in order to please God instead of depending on **grace** and the power of the Holy Spirit. It is also called **legalism.** People who are religious often do not perceive fresh and new ways in which the Holy Spirit wants to move. See also **New Wine**

Renewing of the Mind: See **Meditation.**

Repentance: The word repent means to change one's mind or thinking, as opposed to turning away from certain actions. The word in Greek is *metanoia* and actually means 'to change the thinking that results in changing the behaviour'. In the Hebrew the words *shuv* and *nicham* mean 'to return' and 'to feel sorrow'. Repentance has the meaning of walking in one direction and then making a complete u-turn in order to walk in the opposite direction. It is much more than saying or feeling sorrow. True repentance leads to God-based thinking and ultimately God-based actions (Acts 3: 19; 26: 20; Rom. 12: 2). See also **Holiness; Fear of the Lord/God; Meditation.**

Replacement Theology: This refers to the teaching which states that, the Church of Jesus Christ has completely replaced Israel and the Jewish people in the plans of God on the earth. According to this teaching the purpose and plans of God on the earth will now be seen only through the Church. As a teaching it suggests that God no longer has plans for the Jews and Israel as a nation. In as much as salvation can only come through accepting Jesus Christ as the sin sacrifice, and not through observing the Jewish laws. This teaching is inaccurate because Israel and the Jewish people still have a special place in the heart of God (Ps. 122: 6; Rom. 11: 1–11).

Resurrection life: See *Zoe*

Restoration: This refers to when the Holy Spirit reinstates a certain scriptural truth on earth (Acts 3: 21). For example, the restoration of the prophets and the apostles means these offices are being put in their rightful position and recognition in order to function as God has intended. Restoration can also mean when God gives back to a believer whatever has been lost, stolen or taken by the enemy. Restoration is often given in a greater quantity and quality (Prov. 6:

30–31; Joel 2: 25–26; Luke 4: 18–19; John 10: 10). See also **Present Truth; Third Reformation.**

Revelation: It is *apokalupsis* in the Greek and means 'to make bare' or 'make naked'. It also means to appear, manifest, be uncovered, or be unveiled. Revelation is also called **divine revelation**. A revelation therefore means when the Holy Spirit unveils, manifests or uncovers a particular truth in the scripture or the **spiritual realm**. Revelation is progressive and comes in stages (Acts 26: 16). The more it is pursued, the more it increases. It is the deepest and highest form of understanding God and His Word. The more time spent with a scripture or truth, the more revelation comes from it. Revelation comes from **meditation** and brings **manifestation** (Josh 1: 8–9; Mark 4: 24). When a Scripture has not become revelation it is still *information*, meaning it is in the head of a believer and not the heart or spirit. In this way it cannot be spoken and produce results. Every believer should seek to move in this dimension and trust God for regular revelation because revelation is the source of faith, and faith is the only thing that God can use to bring manifestation of His Word or promises (Matt. 16: 17; Rom. 10: 8–10; 1 Cor. 2: 10; Eph. 3: 3–5). See also **Faith;** *Rhema.*

Revelation Gifts: See **Gifts of the Spirit.**

Revival: This refers to when the Holy Spirit awakens or makes alive either a dormant or non-existent truth in the Scriptures. The word *revive* means 'to bring back to life or to live again'. Revivals are usually characterized by people in a certain area having a greater awareness of God followed by services, soul winning, repentance, intercession, gifts of the Spirit and miracles. **Revivalists** are believers who pioneer or lead revivals.

Revivalists: See **Revival.**

Rhema: A *rhema* word is a word from God which is revealed or spoken by the Holy Spirit to the believer. It refers to a *word that is spoken* rather than a *word that is written*. It is described as a *word from God* as distinguished from a *word of God* (John 14: 26). A *rhema* word is similar to a revelation. A *rhema* word is usually personal whereas the *logos* is general. For example the *logos* will tell a believer to sow financial seed, but the *rhema* will tell the believer where to sow the seed and or what to believe God for. A *rhema* is often contained in prophecies. *See* also **Logos; Revelation.**

Righteousness: It is the Greek word, *dikaios* refers to the state of having 'no sense of shame, guilt or inferiority before God.' Righteousness is the nature of every believer. It has been attained by accepting the blood sacrifice of Jesus Christ. It is the way God sees all believers because all believers have the judicial approval of God. When a believer embraces this truth in their mind they become **righteousness conscience**. The opposite of which is **sin conscience**, which is a state where believers see themselves as falling short of God's grace, forgiveness and love as a result of their sins. Keeping a record of sins when God has forgiven them will prevent the believer from walking in the fullness of what God has for them. All believers must walk in the mind-set of the finished work of the blood of Jesus Christ and in their position of righteousness. **Works of righteousness** refers to all deeds done in accordance with the believer's righteous nature. The only way to stop the sin nature is to awake to the nature of our righteousness (1 Cor. 15: 34; 2 Cor. 5: 17–21; Phil. 3: 9; Heb. 10: 14; 1 John 1: 9). See also **Holiness.**

Royal Priesthood: See **Kings and Priests.**

Running with the Word: See **Standing on the Word.**

Sacrificial Giving: This refers to giving what is of value to God and or His people over and above the **tithe** and **offering** as an act of worship and faith. In Acts the Bible says God was extremely pleased with a man named Cornelius for his sacrificial giving that it became as a memorial to God. This means God took special note of this type of giving, such that He even sent an angel to tell him. Sacrificial giving is uncommon and therefore releases uncommon favour from God (Luke 6: 38, 21: 1–4; John 12: 1–6; Acts: 10: 1–4; 2 Cor. 9: 7; Heb. 13: 16). See also **Giving; Kings; Prosperity.**

Saints: This is one of the tittles and positions given to believers. The word saint comes from the Greek word *hagios*, which means *consecrated to God, holy, sacred*, and *pious*. All believers are saints. The **saints movement** is focused on bringing all believers to this realisation as well as equipping them for the work of their God-given ministry (Acts 9: 13, 32; Eph. 4: 12; 5: 3). See also **Holiness; Fivefold Ministry; Who We Are in Christ.**

Saints of Tribulation: This refers to believers who will be saved during the **Great tribulation**. These people will be left behind at the **rapture** and will only receive **salvation** or repent after it has occurred. The Bible says their salvation will come at a great price and great persecution (Rev. 20: 4). See also **Eschatology.**

Saints Movement: See **Saints**

Salvation: This refers to the state of being saved or delivered from danger, harm, or God's wrath. When a person becomes born-gain or **saved,** they enter into God's salvation. The word salvation is the Greek word *soteria* (taken from *sozo,* meaning 'to rescue'), and it means 'welfare, prosperity, deliverance, preservation, and safety'. God's salvation covers every area of life and not only taking the believer to heaven (Luke 19: 9; Acts 4: 12; Rom. 10: 9–10). See also **Born Again; Sinner's Prayer.**

Salvation Prayer: See **Sinner's Prayer.**

Sanctification: See **Holiness.**

satan/demons: Demons are spirits who were once angels serving God. They led a rebellion against God, which failed. God threw them out of heaven and they have now become fallen angels. They are now operating against God, His Word and believers by influencing people to act against the **Kingdom of God.** The Bible also calls them evil or unclean spirits, devils, principalities, powers, rulers of darkness of this age, spiritual hosts of wickedness in heavenly places, etc. (Matt. 12: 43; Mark 3: 11; Acts 19: 13; Eph. 6: 12). **satan** is the ruler of the demons. The Bible also refers to him as the thief, devil, ancient serpent etc. satan was once a cherub who served God in heaven. Pride overcame him and he rebelled against God together with a third of the angels (now demons). God then cast him out of heaven. (Isa. 14: 6–16; Ezek. 28: 12–19; Luke 10: 18*)*. The devil is a created spirit by God and can therefore never defeat God. Demons can come in many forms, shapes, and sizes but their objective is always to steal, kill, and destroy. (John 10: 10). Believers should therefore learn to keep away from **demonic practices.** Such practices open up **demonic doorways**, or a **legal right for demons** to operate. A legal right for demons is the permission given to demon spirits to operate as a result of violations against the Word of God. The Bible says we should give no place for the devil to operate (Matt. 12: 43–45; Eph. 4: 27; James 4: 7). Believers have complete authority and power over satan and his demons in Jesus Christ, and they should use it regularly. (Mark 16: 17; Luke 10: 19)*See* also **Authority; Deliverance; Demonic Oppression; Spiritual Warfare.**

Saved: See **Salvation.**

School of the Apostles: See **School of the Fivefold Ministries.**

School of the Fivefold Ministries: These are schools set-up to teach, train, activate and release the Fivefold ministers into the Body of Christ. Some may have names like **school of the prophets** or **school of the apostles** (Eph. 4: 11). See also **Fivefold Ministry.**

School of the Holy Spirit: These are schools which seek to manifest the **gifts of the Spirit** through the students they teach. They can also be called **school of the Spirit, training centres** etc. They are different from ordinary Bible schools and seminaries because they emphasise demonstrating the power they are teaching and teach their students how to do the same (1 Cor. 2: 4). See also **Demonstrations of the Holy Spirit; TEAR Programme.**

School of the Prophets: See **School of the Fivefold Ministries.**

School of the Spirit: See **School of the Holy Spirit.**

Season: This refers to a specific time or period on the earth that God has ordained in order to accomplish His plans. The Bible tells us that there is a time and season for everything. For example a believer can go through a season of persecution or go through a season of favour. It is important for every believer to know the season they are in and allow God to manifest His purpose through it (Eccl. 3: 1; Heb. 12: 5–11; 1 Pet. 1: 6–7, 5: 10). See also **Preparation of a Man or Woman of God.**

Second Coming: This refers to the time when Jesus will come to earth with the raptured Church to establish the **millennial rule.** This will happen after the judgement of all those that opposed Him on the earth, and after defeating the Antichrist and False Prophet. It is also known as the **return of the Lord** or the **Lord's day** (Matt. 24: 27; 1 Thess. 3: 13; James 5: 7–9). See also **Eschatology; Rapture: Judgement of God.**

Seed of Abraham: See **Abraham's Blessing.**

Seedtime and Harvest: See **Sowing and Reaping.**

Seeking the Face/Heart of God: This refers to a type of heartfelt prayer and meditation that looks for the guidance, peace, and presence of God. This type of prayer is *intimate, intense, honest* and from the deepest part of the believer. This type of prayer can be contrasted with **seeking the hand of God**, which is the type of prayers and attitude focused on needs and wants, without the desire to connect to God through genuine love and devotion for Him (1 Chron. 16: 11; 22: 19; Ps. 27: 4, 8; Isa. 55: 6; James 4: 8). See also **Praise and Worship; Prayer of Consecration.**

Seeking the Hand of God: See **Seeking the Face/Heart of God.**

Seer: See **Prophet.**

Self-Control/Temperance/Self-Discipline: This is one of the **fruit of the Spirit.** It comes from the Greek word *egkrateia* and means 'having mastery on control over oneself and one's own behaviour' (Prov. 16: 32; 25: 28; 1 Cor. 9: 27; 10: 13; 2 Pet. 1: 5–7). See also **Character.**

Sending Out: See **Commissioning.**

Senior Pastor: See **Pastor.**

Serving in the House: See **Body of Christ.**

Seven Mountain Kingdoms: This refers to the seven major areas of activity, life, or **spheres of influence** on the earth.

(1) Government and law;

(2) Education;

(3) Economy (business & finance);

(4) Family;

(5) Media and communication;

(6) Religion (spirituality and Church); and

(7) Arts and entertainment.

According to the **seven mountain mandate,** all of these areas must be penetrated, influenced, and dominated by the **kingdom of God** through believers before Jesus Christ returns (Gen. 1: 26–27; Deut. 7: 1–2; Matt. 5: 13–16; Luke 10: 19; 1 John 5: 19). See also **End-Time Transfer of Wealth; Joshua Generation; Kings.**

Seven Mountain Mandate: See **Seven Mountain Kingdoms.**

Seven Spheres of Influence: See **Seven Mountain Kingdoms.**

Seven Spirits of God: This refers to the seven ways in which the Holy Spirit reveals His nature. This term does not refer to seven different spirits but rather seven manifestations or characteristics of the Holy Spirit. Just as one God reveals Himself in three ways, so also the one and only Holy Spirit reveals Himself in seven main different ways:

(1) Lord
(2) Wisdom
(3) Understanding
(4) Counsel
(5) Knowledge
(6) Might
(7) Fear of the Lord (Isa. 11: 1–2; Rev. 1: 4). See also **Demonstrations of the Holy Spirit; Fruit of the Spirit; Yielding to the Holy Spirit.**

Sexual Immorality: This refers to any manner of having sexual relations, pleasure or activities outside the permitted boundaries of the Bible. These immoral acts include unmarried believers having sex (**fornication**), married believers having sex with a person other than their spouse (**adultery**), sex with animals or bestiality, sexual pleasure from demons or spirits, pornography, same sex relations or homosexuality, prostitution, orgies or group sex, masturbation, etc. (1 Cor. 6: 18–20; 1 Thess. 4: 3–5; Heb. 13: 4). See also **Holiness; Works/Sins/ Lusts of the Flesh.**

Sheep and Goat Nations: This refers to the overall right or wrong standing of a nation before God. Sheep nations are the nations that God is pleased with and Goat nations are nations which will receive the wrath of God. Every believer must trust and believe God to transform their nation into a Sheep nation for God's glory and not His Judgement (Matt. 25: 31–34). See also **Seven Mountain Kingdoms.**

Shekinah Glory: See **Glory**

Signs and Wonders: This refers to any *unusual, uncommon* or *unnatural* manifestations that happen through the presence and power of God. Signs and wonders are not limited and can mean any way in which God wants to reveal Himself. They are limitless because God is limitless. This term speaks about anything that makes people stand in awe or in wonder of God. The main reason for these signs and wonders is for the unsaved to be convinced that Jesus is who He says He is. Examples of signs and wonders include people being **slain in the Spirit**, the glory of God manifesting, miracles, etc. It can also include **healings, deliverance**, and **creative miracles** (Mark 16: 20; John 21: 25; Heb. 2: 4). See also **Demonstrations of the Holy Spirit; Power Evangelism/Witnessing.**

Sin: Sin can mean several different things:

(1) Miss a mark, goal, or standard.
(2) To breach a relationship, or to rebel.
(3) Perverseness.
(4) An error or mistake.

The most common Greek word is *hamartia*, meaning 'offences against laws, people, or God'. Whichever definition is looked at, they all suggest acts or attitudes that offend God and His Word. Believers have two natures, the **born again** recreated nature (**new man**) and the **sin-nature**. The sin nature is what is called the carnal or flesh nature, which is the inclination of a believer to want to disobey God's Word (Rom. 7: 18–19; Gal. 5: 17). It may not be possible to live a complete sin free life, because of the sin-nature; however, believers must strive for more of the **fruit of the Spirit** daily. Believers must make a decision to forsake all actions, decisions, and environments that promote sin. This can only successfully be done by depending on the nature of the new man and God's **grace**. See also **Holiness; Repentance; Yielding to the Holy Spirit.**

Sin-Nature: See **Sin.**

Sinner's Prayer: This refers to the prayer that leads a person from being a sinner to becoming the righteousness of God in Jesus Christ. It is also called the **salvation prayer** (Rom. 10: 9–10). See also **Believer; Born Again; Salvation.**

Sins of the Heart: See **Inner Healing.**

Slain in the Spirit: It refers to a situation where a person or believer has been knocked down or has fallen under the power of the Holy Spirit. It can also be called **falling under the power** (John 18: 6). See also **Operations of the Holy Spirit.**

Sons of God: This refers to the position believers have been given by God as sons and daughters of God. It is a position of **sonship.** It relates to the Father and child relationship that each believer has with God. Sonship has *nothing to do with gender, race, or age.* Just as Jesus has this relationship with the Father, even so all believers are called sons of God. This is a position of inheritance that all believers enjoy in the kingdom of God. We have been given the right to share in all things with Jesus Christ; this is why the Bible also refers to believers as **heirs** and **joint or coheirs** with Christ. (Rom. 8: 17).

Two words translate 'sons' in the New Testament. The word *technon* refers to infant, child, or youth, and *hoius* speaks about one grown or developed into maturity. *Hoius* is the type of sons God seeks to raise as the manifest sons of God. Believers who fail to appropriate the truth of sonship suffer from an **orphan spirit/mindset**. This type of thinking is a **stronghold** of the devil that prevents believers from realising their adoption to God the Father (Gal. 4: 6–7; 1 John 3:1–2). See also **Fatherhood; Manifest Sons of God.**

Sonship: See **Sons of God.**

Sorcery: See **Demonic/Forbidden Practices.**

Soul Winning: See **Winning Souls.**

Sound Doctrine/Teaching: See **Doctrine.**

Sowing and Reaping: This refers to the spiritual law set in place by God that is to the effect that whatever is given or sown by a believer and the amount or quantity of it is what will be given back or reaped by the believer. It is also called the law of **seedtime and harvest** or the **law of sowing and reaping** (Gen. 8: 22; Luke 6: 38; 2 Cor. 9: 6–8; Gal. 6: 7–10). See also **Partnership; Sacrificial Giving.**

Sowing into anointing: See **Partnership.**

Speaking life: See **Faith Confessions/Decrees/Declarations.**

Speaking the Word: See **Faith Confessions/Decrees/Declarations.**

Special/Supernatural Faith: See **Faith.**

Specific Will of God: See **Calling.**

Spirit led: See **Yielding to the Holy Spirit.**

Spiritual Accountability: This refers to the responsibility that a believer (usually a leader) owes to those above him or her in **spiritual authority**. This responsibility involves being accountable for actions, words and lifestyle. Spiritual authority is a structure that reduces mistakes and any improper conduct according to the Word of God. All believers and leaders especially those in ministry must strive to have matured **elders** to exercise oversight in their lives, especially those in ministry. Having accountability has many advantages, including

(1) Providing **spiritual covering**.
(2) Preventing disunity and fragmentation in the **Body of Christ** and promoting the unity of the Church.
(3) Allowing believers to be **commissioned** and **ordained** in the proper way and timing of God.
(4) Preventing believers and leaders from falling into error and deception.

See also **Apostolic and Prophetic Order; Spiritual Authority; Spiritual Parents.**

Spiritual Authority: This refers to the people whom God has placed over others by virtue of their position and offices in the local Church and in the Body of Christ. **Submission to spiritual authority** refers to the decisions and actions taken by a believer in order to obey, serve and promote the interests and instructions of those in spiritual authority over him or her. See also **Apostolic and Prophetic Order; Elders; Fivefold Ministry; Spiritual Parents.**

Spiritual Covering: See **Covering.**

Spiritual Father or Mother: See **Spiritual Parents.**

Spiritual Gifts: See **Gifts of the Spirit.**

Spiritual Growth: See **Spiritual Maturity.**

Spiritual Maturity: This refers to the development in the spirit and mind of a believer as a result of the Word of God and other spiritual activities or exercises, (1 Tim. 4: 8), such as **fasting** and **prayer.** Spiritual maturity can also be evidenced by outward behaviour. It can also be called **spiritual growth**. It is God's desire for all believers to attain spiritual growth and maturity. The believer will never stop growing because Jesus Christ is the model of growth and He is infinite (1 Cor. 13: 11; 14: 20; Eph. 4: 11–16; Heb. 5: 12–14; 6: 1–2; 1 Pet. 2: 1–2). See also **Character; Fruit of the Spirit; Sons of God.**

Spiritual Mentoring: This refers to the process of providing guidance and grooming by a spiritual elder to another in order to shape and develop the learner into what God has called them to be. This type of mentoring is based on a relationship which involves a mentor using the principles of the Word of God in order to give direction to those under him or her. This process can also be called **Discipling/ Discipleship** (Prov. 27: 17; 2 Tim. 2: 2; Titus 2: 3–5). See also **Fatherhood; Spiritual Parents; Training.**

Spiritual Parents: This refers to those that have and are still contributing the most to the **spiritual growth** of a believer. They can also be called a **spiritual father** and or **mother** (1 Cor. 4: 14–15). See also **Spiritual Authority.**

Spiritual Realm: This refers to the unseen world that co-exists with the natural world where angels, demons and God exist. It can also be called the **realm of the Spirit**. There are three main levels that are recognized in the spiritual realm: From beneath the earth to the sky; in the sky heaven or outer space; and the third and highest realm is heaven, where God and His angels dwell. The realm of the Spirit is accessed through faith in God or through fear in the lies of the devil. Believers can bring the manifestation of their faith or their fears, depending on which voices they are listening to in the spiritual realm (Acts 1: 9–11; Eph. 1: 3; 6: 12). See also **Angelic Ministry; Faith; Satan/Demons.**

Spiritual Warfare: This refers to battles that takes place in the **spiritual realm** between the **kingdom of darkness** and God, His angels, and believers. Believers have been equipped with the **whole armour or God** (Eph. 6: 11–18), which include

- Truth of the Bible
- Righteousness found in Christ Jesus
- Readiness to preach the gospel of Jesus Christ
- Faith in God
- Salvation
- Word of God
- Prayers and supplication in the Spirit.

Believers have also been equipped with **weapons of warfare** found in God (2 Cor. 10: 4–5). These include:

- **Prayer**
- **Pleading the blood** of Jesus Christ
- **Angelic Ministry**
- **Fasting**
- **Speaking the Word**

Stand in the Gap: See **Intercession.**

Standing on the Word: This refers to the faith a believer puts on a *logos* or *rhema* Word of God which may include **personal prophecies**. This is done until its fulfilment is seen. This may also be called *running with the Word*, but this may apply more to a *rhema* word from the Lord. See also **Faith.**

Steward: This refers to the position that a believer has been placed on the earth for in order to manage certain things on behalf of God. This is a position of **stewardship**. There are two words in the Greek for steward translated in the Bible, one is *epitropos*, which means 'to manage', or 'a foreman'. The other is *oikonomos*, which means a 'manager' or 'administrator' of a household. God has placed believers as stewards over the **tithe**, their finances, their health, time, their ministry and the earth. Believers should look at themselves as only mere managers of things that are owned by God. It should therefore never be a problem if God requires believers to give or sacrifice anything that belongs to Him (Gen. 1: 28; 2: 15: Matt. 6: 24; Luke 16: 11; 1 Cor. 6: 19–20). See also **Sacrificial Giving.**

Stewardship: See **Steward.**

Strongholds: In the ordinary sense a stronghold can refer to a *fortress* or *fortified place* where a person or people have *refuge* and *protection*. **Demonic strongholds** therefore would refer to the area in our lives and in the spiritual realm where satan and his demons have found refuge or a place to operate. These are also called bondages. Demonic strongholds within a person come as a result of lies and deception the devil has made a person believe over time. **Tearing down** or **pulling down strongholds** has two main meanings:

(1) The process in which the Word or truth of God is used to break the lies and deception of the enemy and thereby

bringing deliverance to the mind, soul, and spirit of a *person* and;

(2) The process in which believers engage in **spiritual warfare** to frustrate, break up or disturb demon spirits operating in a certain *place* or *territory*. These demons over territories are called **territorial spirits** or **regional spirits** (Rom. 12: 2; 2 Cor. 10: 4–6). See also **Deliverance.**

Submitting to Spiritual Authority: See **Spiritual Authority.**

Submitting to the Holy Spirit: See **Yielding to the Holy Spirit.**

Supernatural Boldness: This refers to the boldness or courage given by the Holy Spirit to a believer in order to accomplish His Word through the believer. This type of boldness is necessary when a believer wishes to manifest **signs and wonders**, especially if the environment is in a non-church area with unbelievers. Believers must learn to constantly ask the Holy Spirit for this boldness. This boldness will not only remove fear from the believer but it will also quicken his or her faith to manifest the supernatural power of God (Deut. 31: 6; Prov. 28: 1; 1 Cor. 16: 13; 2 Tim. 1: 7). See also **Faith; Fear.**

Supernatural: It means to be or being *above* and *beyond* that which is natural. It also means *abnormal* or *extraordinary*. It refers to that which cannot be understood or explained by natural reasoning and human wisdom. *Natural* is defined as, in conformity with the ordinary course of nature; not unusual or exceptional or that which can be experienced by the five senses, understood by the mind, or explained by human reasoning. Although this definition focuses on the supernatural as given by God, it is important to note that, there are *two sources* of the supernatural. It may come from **satan** and his

demons, often seen in **magic/witchcraft/sorcery** (Acts 8: 9–11; 16: 16–19; 2 Cor. 11: 14) and in other **false religions.** The other source is God working through the Holy Spirit and the Word. The believer must ensure to always seek the true source of the supernatural which is God. The **anointing** or **gifts of the Holy Spirit** and the **grace** of God are all supernatural because all of them come from God's ability in us and none of our own abilities. **Releasing the supernatural** refers to any action of faith, followed by a physical manifestation done by a believer in order to demonstrate the power of the Holy Spirit. **Activating the supernatural** refers to the stirring up of the gifts of the Holy Spirit within the believer in order for them to outwardly or physically display this supernatural power of God. This outward display of the power of Holy Spirit is also called **walking in the supernatural power of God.** See also **Demonstrations of the Holy Spirit; Miracles; Spiritual Realm.**

TEAR Programme: This acronym stands for Training by Equipping, Activating, and Releasing. It is premised or based on the mandate given in Eph. 4: 11–16 for the Fivefold ministry. The focus of this programme is to train all believers by equipping them with the truth of their calling and the gifts on their lives, by using both the *logos* and *rhema* Word of God. This process of **equipping** involves a lot of teaching from the Bible and prophecies over a believer. The next step is **activation** which involves activating or imparting the gifts and calling on the person being trained by the trainer. The last step is the **releasing** of the believer to walk in these gifts and callings and for them to then train, equip, activate and release other believers. This is a continual process until all saints are perfected. See also **Fivefold Mnistry; Training; School of the Spirit.**

Taking up the Mantle: See Mantle.

Talents: See Gifts of the Spirit.

Teacher: This is one of the Fivefold ministries mentioned in Eph. 4: 11. The word teacher comes from the Greek word *didaskalos*, which means an 'instructor', a 'tutor', or a 'mentor'. It can also be loosely translated from the word *rabbi* in the Hebrew. Teachers have the unique ability given by God to lay down Biblical concepts *line upon* *line* and *precept upon precept* (Isa. 28: 10), which are easily understood and accepted by the people who hear them. Teachers must themselves be trained in **sound doctrine** in order to correctly teach others (2 Tim. 2: 15; James 3: 1). False teachings refer to doctrine that is erroneous (Acts 13: 1; Rom. 12: 7; Heb. 5: 12). See also **Extremes; Fivefold Ministry; Teaching.**

Teaching: It can refer to a sermon or a teaching given by a believer. The **gift of teaching** is one of the gifts of the Holy Spirit mentioned in Rom. 12: 7. It is the grace given to a believer to teach the Word of God. When a believer is under this grace the Holy Spirit moves with his or her words to bring clarity and understanding to the listeners. The scriptures become *revelation* instead of only mere *information*. This gift enables a believer to bring forth the Word with ease and lay in the spirit of those who are being taught line upon line and precept upon precept. When this gift has matured it can develop into the office of the *teacher* (Eph. 4: 11). See also **Doctrine; Extremes.**

Tearing Down/Pulling Down Strongholds: See **Strongholds.**

Temptation: See **Trials/Tests/Tribulations/Sufferings.**

Territorial Spirits: See **Strongholds.**

Testing the Spirits: See **False/Lying Signs and Wonders.**

Tests: See **Trials/Tests/Tribulations/Sufferings.**

The Curse: See **The Blessing.**

The Law: See **Grace.**

Third Day: It is also called the *latter days* and refers to the season or period which will usher in the coming of Jesus Christ. This period is expected by believers to come with a mighty move of the Holy Spirit resulting in an explosion of His gifts and power and therefore bringing many to Jesus Christ. It will also be a time when the world becomes more evil. This last move of the Spirit is also called the **final wave, third wave, latter wave**, etc. (Hos. 6: 1–3). See also **Eschatology; Rapture.**

Third Reformation: This refers to the final and last stage for which the Church is being prepared to eventually move into. It has been revealed through some prophets that since 2008 this reformation has begun and will continue until the kingdoms of this world have become the kingdoms of the Lord Jesus Christ. The third reformation is premised on the belief that there are still prophetic scriptures yet to be fulfilled before the coming of Christ. These scriptures include the promise of the Church to move into maturity resulting in kingdom **authority** and **dominion** (Dan. 7: 14, 18, 22, 26–27; Acts 3: 21; Rev. 11: 15). Third reformer or reformation anointing is the grace given to certain believers to bring about this reality. (The first Church reformation occurred from the birth of Christ until 313 AD. After this, the church entered the dark ages. The second reformation occurred between 1517 and 2007.) See also **Seven mountain Kingdoms; Restoration.**

Third Wave: See **Third Day.**

Time of Preparation: See **Preparation of a Man or Woman of God.**

Tithe: This refers to the tenth or ten per cent (10%) of whatever income which comes to a believer. The tithe is given to God as an act of worship and honour for His provision. Tithing is not an option for believers. Instead it is a spiritual law that carries consequences with non-compliance. The tithe is usually given into the **local church**. Like **fasting** there is no specific command from God in the New Testament to tithe, but it is a principle that must be followed especially as the seed of Abraham, because we follow in Abraham's footsteps. Tithing is a concept before the Old Testament and the law and is very much alive in the New Covenant and should be practiced by all who claim Jesus Christ as their Lord and High Priest (Gen. 14: 18–20; Mal. 3: 8–12; Heb. 7: 1–9,20–24). See also **First Fruits; Giving; Steward.**

Training: It refers to the process by which a believer is taught aspects of the gifts or calling of God and then activated in the gift or calling through **impartation** and **activation**. There are four main objectives behind training:

(1) To develop **spiritual maturity** in the believer
(2) To place the believer in a position where they can serve God through their gifts and fulfil their **membership role** in the Body of Christ;
(3) To release the believer to function in the **manifestation** of that gift or calling and not only have information or even revelation about it; and
(4) To enable that believer to be able to equip, activate, and train others to move in the gifts and calling of God on their lives (Rom. 1: 11; 11: 29; Eph. 4: 11–16; 2 Tim. 1: 9). See also **Fivefold Ministries; School of the Holy Spirit; TEAR Programme.**

Training Centres: See **School of the Holy Spirit.**

Trance: This refers to a deeper and more intense form of a vision. In a trance the physical senses often become un-operational, and the spirit becomes open to receive a message from God in pictures and words. (Acts 10:10-16). See also **Prophetic Gifts; Vision**

Translation/Transportation: This refers to the supernatural transportation or movement of an object or human from one place to another (Acts 8: 39–40). See also **Miracles; Supernatural.**

Trinity: See **Godhead/Trinity.**

Trials/Tests/Tribulations/Sufferings: These are challenging situations permitted by God in the life of a believer. Challenges of different kinds are in the will of God for every believer. However the intention of trials is always to build the necessary faith and character within a believer in order for God to promote them. Trials are used by God for the following reasons:

(1) To *put a demand on the faith* of a believer, causing them to respond according to His Word (James 1: 2–4; 1 Pet. 1: 6–7).
(2) To teach *discipline* (Heb. 12: 2–11) and *humility* (Deut. 8: 2–3).
(3) To build the *fruit of the Spirit* and godly character (Rom. 5: 3–5; James 1: 2–4).
(4) To reveal *motives and sins of the heart* (Ps. 139: 23–24).

Trials may come in the form of **persecution**, which involves the harassment, affliction, or opposition of a believer because of his or her beliefs. This may come in the form of criticism, violence, and even death. All believers must face persecution in some form (John 15: 19; 2 Tim. 3: 12; 1 John 3: 13). However, those who lead others or pioneer new moves of the Holy Spirit often receive more of it.

The response to persecution is always the fruit of *love* and prayer (Matt. 5: 44; Rom. 12:17). Believers must trust God to fight battles of persecution on their behalf (Rom. 12: 17–21; 1 Pet. 4: 4–5). The trials which God permits, in whichever way they may come are never meant to lead a believer to fail or place them in position of defeat, sin or hopelessness. Instead God delights in the believer's victory every time, in fact it is His will (Ps. 34: 19; 2 Cor. 2: 14).

The opposite of this is true from temptation, which is a situation created by *satan* or his *demons*, intended for the believer's destruction or for them to sin or fail. *Temptations are never from God* (James 1: 13). No matter the trial, the result will always be for the good of a believer if he or she responds according to the principles of the Word, for example faith, rejoicing, sowing seed, etc. (Rom. 8: 28, 35–39). His **grace** is always available to overcome any trial or temptation (1 Cor. 10: 13; 2 Cor. 12: 9; Phil. 4: 13). See also **Character; Faith; Preparation of a Man or Woman of God; Seasons.**

Two Witnesses: This refers to two men who will be sent by God from heaven to earth. These two witnesses of God will have the power to prevent it from raining on the earth, to call fire down from heaven, to turn bodies of water into blood, and to command a number of other plagues, as signs of God's existence and coming wrath. After they preach for forty-two months, the **antichrist** will be allowed to kill them. Three and a half days later they will be resurrected and Raptured up to heaven. Some scholars say the two men could either be Elijah and Enoch; or Moses and Elijah (Mal. 4: 5–6; Rev. 11: 3–13). See also **Eschatology.**

Types of Prophets: See **Prophets.**

Unbelief: See **Faith.**

Unction of the Holy Spirit: See **Anointing**

Unforgiveness: This refers to the state of the heart and mind of a believer to refuse to let go or pardon another person for a wrong they have done to them. Unforgiveness can also be directed towards God where a person feels hurt by God for areas such as unanswered prayers, failures in life, tragic occurrences etc. Believers must be open enough with God and tell Him where they feel He has failed them and then ask Him to remove what they feel toward Him.

Unforgiveness can have the following effects on a believers' lives:

(1) Hinder their faith and prevent answers to payer.
(2) Deny them God's forgiveness of their sins and eventually lead them to hell.
(3) Cause illness and physical ailments.
(4) Bring demonic oppression and attacks.
(5) Cause depression, stress, and anxiety. In order to forgive, believers must *decide* to forgive and then *depend* on God to help them (Matt 6: 12; Mark 11: 23–26; John 20: 23; Rom. 12: 14; Eph. 4: 26–27, 32; 1 John 1: 9; 4: 20). See also **Fruit of the Spirit; Inner Healing; Love.**

Universal Church: See **Church.**

Unmerited Favour: See **Grace.**

Unpardonable Sin: It also called the unforgivable sin. It refers to the wilful and intentional degrading or cursing of God or things attributed to God. God can forgive all sins, except for this one according to the Bible. It is unclear exactly what this sin is. It is commonly believed to be the turning away of a firm believer from Christ (Matt. 12: 31–32; Mark 3: 28–30).

Unsound Doctrine: See **Doctrine**

Utterance Gifts: See **Gifts of the Spirit.**

Vision: This refers to the communication given by God to a person through pictures (*stationary or moving*) and sometimes words while the person is awake. An **open-eye vision** or an **open vision** refers to a vision that is given while the person has their physical eyes opened (Acts 7: 55–56). A **closed vision** or **closed-eye vision** refers to a vision that is given while the person has his or her eyes closed (Dan. 8: 1–27; Acts 2: 17). See also **Dream; Trance; Visitation.**

Visitation refers to the manifestation of an angel or God appearing to a human being. Visitations are called as such because generally angels and God live in the **spiritual realm** and not in the natural realm. Demonic visitations cannot be regarded as falling within this definition because they are unwanted and unwelcome and generally have no right to be near or around believers unless given permission. Visitations can come through or in the form of **dreams, visions, trances,** or actual manifestation while a believer is in their natural state of body and mind (Luke 1: 26–37; Acts 10: 3–7; 27: 23–24; Heb. 13: 2). See also **Angelic Ministry.**

Walking in the Spirit: See **Yielding to the Holy Spirit.**

Waiting on God: See **God's Timing.**

Walking in the Supernatural: See **Supernatural.**

Wealth Transfer: See **End-Time Transfer of Wealth.**

Who We Are in Christ Jesus: This refers to the various *positions*, *titles*, and *natures* that *all* believers have been given by God as a result of being *born again*. They include but are not limited to **sons of God, saints, kings, priests; royal priesthood; heirs, joint/coheirs, new creation, ambassadors, His Body, His Church** etc. Each position has its unique anointing, and believers will function in the grace of whichever position they receive revelation of the most.

Whole Armour of God: See **Spiritual Warfare.**

Wilderness Experience/Period: This refers to a period of time in a believer's life which brings with it trials and challenging situations. This term can more commonly be used to mean a period of preparation and testing by God. It is not uncommon for believers to experience this period before God releases a **breakthrough** (Deut. 8: 2–3; Matt. 4: 1–11). See also **Preparation of Man or Woman of God; Season; Trials/Tests/Tribulations/Sufferings.**

Will of God: See **Calling.**

Winning Souls: This refers to the witnessing or telling unbelievers about the cross of Jesus Christ and then leading them to salvation through prayer. This is also called leading people into salvation or *soul winning* or *winning the lost.* Winning souls is the primary duty of every believer (Prov. 11: 30; Matt. 28: 19). See also **Born Again; End-Time Transfer; Great Commission; Power Evangelism/ Witnessing; Salvation; Sinner's Prayer.**

Word of God: See *Logos.*

Word of Knowledge: This is when Holy Spirit reveals the *past* or *present* facts about a person, place or situation. It may include names, numbers or any other information. It is different from human knowledge because the information that comes is unknown to the person giving it until God reveals it (2 Kin. 5: 26; John 4: 17–18). See also **Prophetic Gifts.**

Word of Wisdom: This is when the Holy Spirit reveals the *guidance* and *direction* needed in order to solve a particular problem. It is a God inspired way to solve problems. It is different from human wisdom because the word of wisdom comes directly from God to solve a problem, and not from the natural mind. God usually reveals a situation through the **word of knowledge** and then gives the solution through a word of wisdom (Gen. 41: 34–35). See also **Prophetic Gifts.**

Works/Sins/Lusts of the Flesh: This refers to some sins that are listed in Gal. 5: 19–21. They are sins which the *sin-nature* of a believer produces when it is given permission to do so, and not controlled through the recreated **born-again** nature and the Holy

Spirit. The process of walking in the nature of the born-again spirit and forsaking lusts of the flesh is called **crucifying the flesh** (Gal. 5:24; Col. 3:5). These sins include **adultery, fornication**, uncleanness, **lewdness, idolatry, sorcery**, hatred, contention, jealousy, wrath, selfish ambition, dissension, heresy, envy, murder, drunkenness, and revelry (Rom. 8: 5–10; 1 Cor. 6: 9–11; Gal. 5: 16–21 New King James Version). See also **Fruit of the Spirit; Holiness; Sin; Yielding to the Holy Spirit.**

Works of Righteousness: See **Righteousness.**

Worship: See **Praise and Worship.**

Yielding to the Holy Spirit: It may also be called **submitting to the Holy Spirit,** and it refers to the voluntary decision and action of faith a believer makes in order to allow the Holy Spirit to lead, direct, and flow through him or her. This is what is referred to as **walking in the Spirit**. Believers must make an effort to regularly *invite* the Holy Spirit to manifest His nature, His gifts and His Fruit in their lives. This will also result in the **leading of the Holy Spirit** or being **Spirit-led**, which essentially is the direction given to a believer in matters of life by the Holy Spirit (Isa. 11: 1–2; Gal. 5: 16; 22–23). See also **Fruit of the Spirit; Seven Spirits of God.**

-Z-

Zion is used to refer to the hill or mountain in Jerusalem where the city of David was built. It also refers to Jerusalem and Israel as a nation. However Zion can now be used to refer to the Church and the **New Jerusalem** which is to come (Isa. 60: 14; Heb. 12: 22; Rev. 14: 1).

Zoe is the Greek word for *life*, which refers to 'the life of God'. The Zoe life is the very life that God is and has to give away. God is self-existent and needs no other source to keep Him alive, because He is life itself. He is the fullness of life. This life is also called the **resurrection life,** because it can bring anything to life, and it replaces death when in operation. Believers have access to this life and by keeping and speaking the Word of God, they can bring life to anything God permits (John 1: 4, 10: 10, 14: 6).

BIBLIOGRAPHY

Copeland, Kenneth. *The Force of Faith*. Forth, TX, Kenneth Copeland Publications, 2010.

Eckhardt, John. *Ordinary People, Extraordinary Power:* Florida, Charisma House, 2010.

Hamon, Bill. *Apostles, Prophets, and the Coming Moves of God,* Shippensburg, PA: Destiny Image Publications, 1997.

Hamon, Bill. *Prophetic Scriptures Yet to Be Fulfilled.* Shippensburg, PA: Destiny Image Publications. 2010.

Jacobs, Cindy. *Possessing the Gates of the Enemy.* Michigan Chosen. 1994

Jeffrey, Grant R., ed. *NIV Prophecy Marked Reference Study Bible.* Zondervan, 1999.

Jonathan, David. *Apostolic Strategies Affecting Nations,* Malaysia Destiny Heights. 1997.

Newman, Bob. *Everything the Bible Says about Angels and Demons* Bethany House Publishers, 2012.

Price, Paula A. *The Prophets Dictionary.* New Kensington PA, Whitaker Publications. 2006.

Rajah, Abraham S. *God Wants You to Prophesy,* Johannesburg South Africa, Trumpet Publications. 2013.

Wagner, C. Peter. *Discover Your Spiritual Gifts.* California USA, Regal Books. 2005.

Websites

www.123hallelujah.wordpress.com.

www.assesme.org.

www.bible.cc.

www.biblesuite.com.

www.discoverrevelation.com.

www.greatbiblestudy.com.

www.openbible.info.

www.webster-dictionary.org.

www.wikipedia.com.

Software

E-sword 7.9.8.

PC – Bibles study 5.

ABOUT THE AUTHOR

Abraham S. Rajah has been raised by God to father and pioneer the *Kings & Priests Movement.* This movement includes the restoration of the apostolic and prophetic ministry. This final move by God will reveal itself through the army prophesied by Joel in the Bible.

He has been graced by God to walk in the offices of apostle, prophet, and teacher. His mandate by God includes raising and activating every believer to walk in his or her calling and in the supernatural power of God evidenced by the gifts of the Holy Spirit, in signs, wonders and miracles.

He completed his diploma at Heritage of Faith Bible Institute of Jerry Savelle Ministries. He is married to his lovely wife, Hephzibah, and both have practiced law for a number of years in private practice.

Their three children, a daughter, Abigail, and two sons, Elijah and Zion Abraham, stay with them in Johannesburg, South Africa, which is also the location of their international ministry.

ABOUT THE KINGS &
PRIESTS MOVEMENT

Abraham S. Rajah has been called to father the kings & priests movement.

The *priests* restoration is focused on identifying, training, and maturing those called into the Fivefold ministry – Apostles, Prophets, Evangelists, Pastors, and Teachers – in order to bring every believer to fulfil his or her role in the Body of Christ.

The *kings* restoration is focused on raising believers who are called to exert dominion over the seven spheres of influence (a.k.a. seven mountain Kingdoms): government, education, economy, family, media, religion, and arts.

This mandate has been prophesied many times over. As a result of this mandate, Abraham has, through the Holy Spirit, developed the TEAR (Training by Equipping, Activating, and Releasing) Programme.

Abraham is the apostle and founder of Kings and Priests International (KPI), a network of churches and ministries. KPI's mantra can be summed up as follows: "Preparing every nation for kingdom demonstration."

He is also the founder of the Kings & Priests Movement Church (KPMC), which is dedicated to the calling and mandate of Kings and Priests.

He and his lovely wife, Hephzibah, run KPI & KPMC together.

BECOME A PARTNER TODAY!

Help Kings & Priests International (KPI) take this final move of God around the world.

What is a KPI Partner

- A partner is anyone who makes a decision to support this ministry in finances, prayer and fasting. (The vision of the ministry is on the website for prayer and fasting).
- We at *KPI* believe your tithes belong to your local church.

Why Partner with KPI

- As much as God has given this ministry this unique and extremely important vision, it cannot be done without your help and support. God wants to restore His Church to the place of power and dominion and for His people to move in signs, wonders and miracles as we embrace the Apostolic and Prophetic Movement.
- *KPI* is dedicated to producing books, CDs, DVDs, manuals, and building training centres in Africa and around the world to see the rise of God's Kings and Priests. *(Rev. 5: 10)*.
- We believe your financial needs will be met. We trust God for debt cancellations, business ideas, approved loans etc.

- We believe God will pour on you the signs, wonders and gifts that move with the Apostolic and Prophetic ministry that we are (see Gal. 6: 6–9; Matt. 10: 41; Phil. 4: 16–18; 2 Kings 4: 4–18).
- You get exclusive invites to partner gathering complete with personal prophecies and prayer.
- Not to mention free materials and resources as they become available.

How to Partner with KPI

You can partner financially with **KPI** in the following ways:

- Direct bank deposit
- EFT
- Debit or stop order
- Cheques (written out to Kings and Priests International)
- Paypal / Payfast

When to Partner with KPI

- This is between you and God however we encourage you make a prayerful decision to become a ***monthly partner*** with us. No amount is too small or too big.
- If the Lord has laid in your heart to sow into *KPI*, land, houses, vehicles, jewellery, furniture etc. Please contact us to arrange the logistics.

Partnership information can be found on our website. www.kingspriests.co.za.

Contact Information

To order additional copies of this book or other books, please visit our website for more information: www.kingspriests.co.za.

E-mail: info@kingspriests.co.za
PO Box 783153
Sandton 2146
South Africa

Call centre +27 11 056 5822 /+27 82 2290 370
SMS +27 82 2290 370

INDEX

B

Babylon system 11
Backslider 11
Baptism with fire. *See* Baptism
Baptism with the Holy Spirit. *See*
    Baptism
Believer 12
Bishop 12
Body of Christ 13
Boldness. *See* Supernatural boldness
Bondages. *See* Strongholds
Born-again 13
Break-through 14

C

Calling 15
Carnal believer / Christian 16
Celibacy 16
Cessationism 16
Character 16
Charismatic movement 17
Christ. *See* Anointing
Church 17
Church planting 17
Closed vision / closed eye vision. *See*
    Vision
Coming soon. *See* Prepare the way
Commissioning 18
Compassion / mercy 18
Condemnation 19
Conviction of the Holy Spirit 19
Corporate anointing. *See* Anointing
Covenant 19
Covering 20

Covetousness. *See* Idolatry; *See*
    Idolatry
Creative miracles 20
Crucifying the flesh. *See* Works / sins
    / lusts of the flesh
curse of the Law. *See* Abraham's
    blessings

D

Day of the Lord. *See* End-times
Deacon 22
Debauchery / lasciviousness 22
Deliverance 24
Deliverance minister. *See* Deliverance
Deliverance ministry. *See* Deliverance
Demon / devil consciousness 22
Demonic / forbidden practices 23
Demonic oppression 25
Demonic strongholds. *See*
    Strongholds
Demons. *See* satan / demons
Demonstration of Power. *See*
    Demonstrations of the Holy
    Spirit
Demonstrations of the Holy Spirit 25
Descension gifts. *See* Gifts of the
    Spirit
Dimension 26
Discerning of spirits 26
Discipling / discipleship. *See*
    Sipiritual mentoring
Divination. *See* Demonic / forbidden
    practices
Divine revelation. *See* Revelation
Doctrine 26
Dominion 27

J

Jehohav-Nissi. *See* Names of God

Jehovah-Jireh. *See* Names of God

Jehovah-Maccaddeshem. *See* Names of God

Jehovah-Rapha. *See* Names of God

Jehovah-Rohi. *See* Names of God

Jehovah-Sabbaoth. *See* Names of God

Jehovah-Shalom. *See* Names of God

Jehovah-Shamah. *See* Names of God

Jehovah-Tsidkenu. *See* Names of God

Jehovah / Yahweh. *See* Names of God

Jezebel spirit 56

Joshua assignment / mandate. *See* Joshua generation

Joshua generation 57

Judgement of believers. *See* Judgement of God

Judgement of God 58

Judgement Seat of Christ. *See* Juudgement of God

Justification. *See* Holiness

K

Kindness 59

Kingdom building 59

Kingdom now. *See* Kingdom of God

Kingdom now movement. *See* Kingdom of God

Kingdom of darkness 60

Kingdom of God 60

Kingdom of God movement. *See* Kingdom of God

Kingdom owned businesses. *See* Kingdom owned businesses

Kingly believer 60

Kings 62

Kings and priests 61

Kings and priests movement. *See* Kings and priests

L

Last hour / days. *See* End-times

Latter day. *See* Latter rain

Latter day saints. *See* Latter rain

Latter rain 63

Latter rain movement. *See* Latter rain

Latter wave. *See* Third day

Law of sowing and reaping. *See* Sowing and reaping

Laying on of hands 64

Leadership 64

Leading of the Holy Spirit. *See* Yielding to the Holy Spirit

Legalism. *See* Religious spirit

Legal right. *See* Inner-healing

Lewdness. *See* Debauchery / lasciviousness

Local church. *See* Church

Logos 65

Longsuffering. *See* Patience / longsuffering

Love 65

M

Magic / witchcraft / sorcery. *See* Demonic / forbidden practices

Mandate. *See* Calling

Manifestation 66

Manifest sons of God 66

Manifest sons of God movement. *See*
    Manifest sons of God
Mantle 66
Many are called but few are chosen.
    See Preparation of a man /
    woman of God
Marketplace 67
Marriage supper of the Lamb 68
Meditation 68
Membership role / ministry\. *See*
    Body of Christ
Message. *See* Message
Mid-tribulation rapture. *See* Rapture
Millennial era 69
Millennial kingdom. *See*
    Millenial era
Millennial rule. *See* Millenial era
Minister. *See* Ministry
Ministry 69
Miracle 70
Miracle money / wealth 70
Movement 70

N

Nabi. *See* Prophet
Names of God. *See* Names of God
Networking. *See* Apostolic and
    prophetic networking
Networks 75
New Age 75
New covenant. *See* Covenant
New creation. *See* Born-again
New Jerusalem 75
New man\. *See* Born-again
New-truths. *See* Present truths
New Wine 75

New Wine movement. *See* New Wine

O

Occult 77
Offering 77
Old covenant. *See* Covenant
Omega-generation 77
Omni-attributes of God 77
Omnipotent. *See* Omni-attributes
    of God
Omnipresent. *See* Omni-attributes
    of God
Omniscient. *See* Omni-attributes
    of God
Once saved always saved 78
Open doors 78
Open eye vision / open vision. *See*
    Vision
Open Heaven. *See* Glory
Operation of the Holy Spirit 79
Ordination 79
Original sin. *See* Fall of man
Orphan spirit / mindset. *See* Sons
    of God

P

Parakletos. *See* Exhort / exhortation
Partner. *See* Partnership / partnering
Partnership / partnering 80
Pastor 80
Patience / longsuffering 81
Paying the price for the calling\ 81
Peace 81
Pentecostal movement. *See*
    Movement

R

Redeemed from the curse of the Law. *See* Abraham's blessing

Regional spirits. *See* Strongholds

Releasing. *See* T.E.A.R Programme

Releasing the supernatural. *See* Supernatural

Religious spirit 95

Renewing of the mind. *See* Meditation

Repentance 96

Replacement theology 96

Restoration 96

Revelation 97

Revelation gifts. *See* Gifts of the Spirit

Revival 97

Revivalists. *See* Revival

Rhema 98

Righteousness 98

Royal priesthood. *See* Kings and priests

Running with the Word. *See* Standing on the Word

S

Sacrificial giving 99

Saints 99

Saints movement. *See* Saints

Saints of tribulation 99

Salvation 100

Salvation prayer. *See* Sinner's prayer

Sanctification. *See* Holiness

satan / demons 100

Saved. *See* Salvation

School of the apostles. *See* School of the Fivefold ministries

School of the Fivefold ministries 101

School of the Holy Spirit 101

School of the prophets. *See* School of the Fivefold ministries

School of the Spirit. *See* School of the Holy Spirit

Season 101

Second Coming 102

seed of Abraham. *See* Abraham's blessings

Seedtime and harvest. *See* Sowing and reaping

Seeking the face / heart of God 102

Seeking the hand of God. *See* Seeking the face / heart of God

Seer. *See* Prophet

Self-control / temperance / self-discipline 103

Sending out 103

Senior pastor. *See* Pastor

Serving in the House. *See* Membership role / ministry

Seven mountain kingdoms 103

Seven mountain mandate. *See* Seven mountain kingdoms

Seven spheres of influence. *See* Seven mountain kingdoms

Seven Spirits of God 104

Sexual immorality 104

Sheep and Goat nations 104

Signs and wonders 105

Sin-nature. *See* Sin

Sinner's prayer 106

Sins of the heart. *See* Inner-healing

Slain in the Spirit 106

Sonship. *See* Sons of God

Kings & Priests Are Social – Are You?

Facebook:apostle&prophetabrahamsrajah
Twitter:@kingspriests
Youtube

INVITATIONS / SPEAKING OPPORTUNITIES

To invite the author to preach or teach at your church, conference, or Bible school, please visit our website, www.kingspriests.co.za, or e-mail info@kingspriests.co.za.

We are walking your journey with you.
Send us your deepest prayer request!

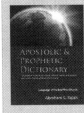

Precious believer, my wife, Prophetess Hephzibah and I want to stand with you for your most urgent needs. Whether you need breakthrough in finances, marriage, demonic oppression, depression, direction, or anything else – *we mean anything* – send your request via our many social applications or to prayer@kingspriests.co.za.

Don't forget to send us your testimony. We know God will do something amazing in your life once we release our faith together.

We love you and are waiting to hear from you.

Printed in the United States
by Baker & Taylor Publisher Services